NECESSARY
HERESIES

ALTERNATIVES TO
FUNDAMENTALISM

Published by
NEW SOUTH WALES UNIVERSITY PRESS
PO Box 1 Kensington NSW Australia 2033
Telephone (02) 398 8900
Fax (02) 398 3408

First published 1993

National Library of Australia
Cataloguing-in-Publication entry:

Cameron, Peter, 1945–   .
  Necessary heresies: alternatives to fundamentalism.

  Bibliography.
  Includes index.
  ISBN 0 86840 293 1.

  1. Modernist—fundamentalist controversy. I. Title.

273.9

Printed by Southwood Press, Marrickville, NSW

Available in North America through:
ISBS Inc
Portland Oregon 97213-3644
Tel: (503) 287 3093
Fax: (503) 280 8832

PETER CAMERON

NECESSARY
HERESIES

ALTERNATIVES TO
FUNDAMENTALISM

PRESS

Contents

Contents

Introduction

$\mathcal{I}$N March 1992 I gave an address, in a Sydney church, on the place of women in Christianity (the first address in the present collection). Some people took exception to the content of that address; official complaints were made; an inquiry was ordered, followed by a 'judicial process'; and eventually, in March 1993, the Sydney Presbytery of the Presbyterian Church of Australia found me guilty of heresy — the sentence is yet to be determined.

The precise charge (although 'precise' may not be the best word) was that I had made public statements inconsistent with Chapter 1 of the Westminster Confession of Faith. In effect this meant that I had challenged the authority and infallibility of the Bible.

The case has attracted an extraordinary amount of media attention — quite disproportionate, one might think, to its apparent importance. Considered narrowly, after all, it merely involves the status of one minister in a denomination with a membership of around 40,000.

There are probably two reasons for this exaggerated public interest. The first is the natural curiosity aroused by anything out of the ordinary, especially when it has been out of the ordinary for several hundred years. It's almost as if the dodo had been discovered to be alive and well, or as if businessmen had started going to work again on horseback. But the second reason is more interesting. There is a feeling, I think, that something significant is involved, something much wider in its implications than simply a parochial matter of ecclesiastical discipline, and something much more sinister than simply a quaint resurrection of archaic customs.

I refer of course to the phenomenon of Fundamentalism. There is no doubt that my accusers are Fundamentalists; indeed it is unlikely that they would deny this, although they might prefer a euphemism like 'conservative evangelicals'. The distinctive characteristics of Fundamentalism are an alleged belief in the literal infallibility of the Bible and an unwillingness to allow that anyone who does not share this belief is entitled to be called a Christian, both of which characteristics are conspicuous in the present case.

And Fundamentalism is unfortunately rife in the Presbyterian Church of Australia, which has almost reached the stage of repudiating its presbyterian inheritance altogether — if intellectual rigour and a respect for the plain man's views are taken to be the distinguishing marks of that inheritance.

But the Fundamentalist phenomenon is not confined to the Presbyterian Church of Australia: it is widespread in the Anglican community, and on the increase in most other denominations. And it is not confined to the Christian Church. It seems in fact to be a sign of our times. The reason for its attraction is presumably a desire for certainty in an uncertain world, and for the feeling of security which obedience to a rule-book brings — an illusory certainty, naturally, and a spurious security, but then honesty is not on the agenda.

What is on the agenda is the gradual elimination of individuality and intellectual freedom. Of course, taken by himself (and it is almost always a 'he') there is nothing at all sinister about the Fundamentalist. His motives — more authority and influence for himself — are usually transparent, and his mental equipment is usually sparse. But collectively it is a different matter. I am increasingly convinced that, collectively, Fundamentalism is a major threat to civilisation, comparable on the moral and intellectual plane to the physical threat posed by AIDS. (And like AIDS it seems to spread most easily and rapidly among the young.) Totalitarianism in any form is a great evil, but the religious kind is the worst.

7

It is this threat, I think, that people recognise behind the present process, although they may not be in a position to articulate their fears. And it is in order to help them to articulate their fears that this book has been published. The purpose is simply to alert people to what is going on, not only in the Presbyterian Church of Australia but in every church, and to indicate some of the ways in which Fundamentalism is both dangerous and absurd.

The book is a collection of addresses. (I find that people are reluctant for some reason to concede to any of my addresses the title 'sermon'.) Roughly a third of them were given in St Andrew's College in the University of Sydney, some in schools or as graduation addresses, and the rest in St Philip's Church in Edinburgh. The odd topical or temporal reference has been left unedited — it should be fairly obvious where and when each address originated. And once or twice the same illustration resurfaces. There is a story about a minister in Scotland in the eighteenth century who survived in his parish for ten years on a repertoire of four sermons. When some of his congregation asked whether they might have more variety he replied: 'My friends, my sermons are intended to do you good. When I see that you practise what I have been preaching for so many years, then I will treat you to something different.' With such a precedent, I make no apology for the occasional doublet.

Women

$\mathcal{I}$ read in a British newspaper some time ago about an army officer who discovered that by a typing error he had been entered in the Gazette as a major with seniority from 1 January in the year 1042. Obviously it was supposed to be 1942, but he immediately applied for back pay in the sum of several hundred thousand pounds. To his astonishment, back came a letter from the Ministry of Defence, informing him that his claim would be allowed. It went on, however, to tell him that as he appeared to be the only surviving officer of the Battle of Hastings in 1066, he was being held personally responsible for the large number of bows, arrows, spears and shields which had been misappropriated on that occasion, the value of which by sheer coincidence was only a few pence more than the sum he had claimed as back pay. In the circumstances both parties agreed to forget the matter.

It reminded me of the story of the Cambridge student who discovered an old statute of the University, dating from the fifteenth century, which had never been repealed and which entitled every student sitting a Part I exam to a glass of claret. Armed with this statute, therefore, he went into the examination room, sat down, and demanded a glass of claret before beginning the exam. The invigilator, who happened to be the Professor of Medieval History, immediately arranged for his request to be granted, but at the same time fined the student one guinea for contravening an equally ancient statute which made the wearing of spurs compulsory at all examinations.

The point of these two stories obviously is that it is a mistake to look at the past through rose-coloured spectacles, to glamorise it, to refer to it as 'the good old days', and to ignore all its negative aspects. We all do this of course. We do it in our private lives: when we look back on our children's infancy, we remember all the charming things and forget the nappies and the screams in the night. We do it collectively: a nation doesn't as a rule dwell on its ignominious periods and its spectacular defeats — it concentrates on its heroes and its golden age. It's human nature to forget pain and remember pleasure — it's a kind of survival mechanism.

But it is a tendency which can be harmful because it involves a denial of reality. It's always dangerous to turn your back on reality — and particularly in matters of religion, because religion in any case is always threatening to become a substitute for reality, or at least to lose its connection with reality.

There is a cautionary tale which is relevant here, concerning a guru who lived in India several hundred years ago. This guru owned a cat — to the extent that a guru can be said to own anything, and to the extent that anyone can be said to own a cat. The guru was very fond of the cat, and the cat was very fond of the guru, and whenever the guru went across to the temple to conduct a service, the cat went with him. But after a while this became irritating to the worshippers, because they kept tripping over the cat; so the guru, rather than hurt the cat's feelings by leaving it at home, kept it tied up in a corner of the temple during services. In due course the guru died and his successor, feeling sorry for the cat, continued to allow it to attend the temple services, so long as it was tied up in its corner. But then some time later the cat died; and the worshippers found that they missed its presence during their services, so they got hold of another cat and kept it tied up in the corner.

Three hundred years later, there was still a cat tied up in the corner of that temple during services. No one knew why — even the current guru had no idea of the origin of the tradition — but it was regarded by everyone as an indispensable part of the service. They were incapable of worshipping their god except in the presence of a tied-up cat.

Now it seems to me that certain aspects of Biblical authority are analogous to that tied-up cat. For many people the Bible represents the security of a book which tells them what to think. The New Testament seems to them to be the record of a religious golden age, when the church was strong and united, when people knew what they believed and Christianity was just a question of spreading the good news. And faced with the confusion, the intellectual and moral turmoil of the present age, they shout: 'Let's go back to the Bible, let's go back to the ideals of the early church, let's have a resurgence of Biblical teaching and Biblical values and Biblical authority'.

Now this is fantasy; it's seeing history as all claret and no spurs. You find it most clearly in the way the apostle Paul is appealed to as the supreme authority. But in fact Paul's letters indicate first that the early Christian establishment was very reluctant to grant him any authority at all, and second that he himself was very reluctant to grant any one else any authority. His opponents dismissed him as a charlatan, with no real independent status: they said that his authority was derived from that of the true apostles, and that his teaching was all wrong anyway. In reply, Paul asserted his complete independence from the other apostles and said that his understanding of the gospel was revealed to him directly by the risen Christ.

But what subsequent Christians, our own generation included, have tended to do is simply to accept Paul's conclusions as authoritative and ignore all the struggles which preceded them. We are tempted to see the Bible as the beginning of a process and not as the end. We think of Paul as the divine apostle who simply wrote down what was dictated to him, and we forget that he himself had to work out his own salvation in fear and trembling. Paul had to forge a new language in order to express his own unique religious experience in his own unique contemporary situation. He never intended to say: 'This is how it is, and this is how all Christians will express themselves for the next 2000 years'. So that by appealing to Paul's theological formulations as authoritative, we contradict Paul himself. He didn't appeal to human authority — quite the contrary, he thrashed out his position all by himself. In fact, the irony is that the mentality of those in the present day who appeal to the authority of Paul is exactly the mentality of Paul's first century opponents, who slavishly appealed to the authority of the Jewish law.

Now the relevance of all this is that in 1991 the General Assembly of the Presbyterian Church of Australia voted by about two to one to ban the ordination of women, and one of the ostensible grounds for that decision was a remark in Paul's First Letter to Timothy. The First Letter to Timothy is famous for two passages. One is 5:23: 'No longer drink only water, but take a little wine for the sake of your stomach' — a passage in which generations of conscientious ministers have found consolation. The other is the passage which contains the notorious verse 2:13: 'I permit no woman to teach or to have authority over men; she is to keep silent'.

What are we to say to this, assuming that we are not to keep silent? Well, it is possible to refute the appeal to the authority of the divine apostle by denying that the letters to Timothy were written by Paul in the first place — and there would be a great deal of scholarly weight behind that position. But of course it is impossible to prove that the letters are not by Paul; and in any case, if you believe in the absolute and literal authority of the Bible, then it doesn't matter who wrote the First Letter to Timothy — you are still bound by it. A much better argument, therefore, is to attack the underlying understanding of the Bible.

Let me illustrate this by the not unrelated matter of Paul's extremely hostile attitude to homosexuality. It is possible to rescue Paul, or to rescue homosexuality, depending on how one looks at it, by arguing that what he had in mind was not innate or instinctive homosexual tendencies but the kind of extreme decadence which is sated with normal channels and is looking for some new stimulus. And I think that this is very probably what he did have in mind. But the much more important question is this: even if he was talking about all sorts of homosexuality, does it matter? Are we bound by his views? I think not. It's not simply that his views are time-bound, it is actually possible that he got things wrong. There is no reason why Paul should have been infallible — indeed I should admire him less if he were infallible. You don't learn very much from perfect beings: you learn most from people who are just a little better than yourself.

So much for the status of the argument against the ordination of women: however much people quote I Timothy 2:13, the answer should simply be: 'So what?' But it is obviously not enough just to refute the argument against the ordination of women — that is a purely negative exercise. I myself would want to take a much more positive view and argue for the ordination of women, not on the basis that there is nothing against it, but on the basis that there is a great deal for it.

Now it is possible to do this by appealing to some other passages in the Bible — for example, 'In Christ there is neither male nor female' (which incidentally is also Paul). But that of course is to play the same game, and the exercise degenerates into each side hurling proof texts at the other. Much more important is to listen to the inner logic of Christianity.

What I mean by that is that Christianity is above all a religion of freedom. Freedom is the prerequisite for everything else. You cannot have love without freedom, you can only have fear. You cannot have growth without freedom, you can only have obedience.

Last year I was at a conference of heads of colleges, and one college principal told us that there were never any problems in his college, because they have three simple rules which take care of everything: no alcohol, no noise after 11 p.m., and no sex. In other words, no wine, women or song. And the alarming thing was that this was greeted with enthusiasm and applause by many of the other heads. But a college which operates on the basis of rules like that isn't a college at all: it's a puritanical denial of life. There is in fact a New Puritanism on the prowl in our society, and it has to be resisted. And this decision of the Presbyterian Church against the ordination of women may well be the latest manifestation of just such a New Puritanism.

What it certainly is, is a restriction of Christian liberty. They are saying, these people, that only men have a right to be ministers, or that no one has a right to listen to a female minister. And the simple answer is that they themselves have no right to say such things, and when they do say them they cease to be Christian, because they deny that freedom which is inseparable from Christianity.

Incidentally, it is one thing to look at all this on a purely abstract or theoretical level; and even on that level it's enough to make one hot under the collar. But it was only recently that the full significance came home to me, when I suddenly realised that one effect of the decision to ban the ordination of women is that my daughter cannot become a minister of the Presbyterian Church of Australia. I don't mean that she was intending to; I mean that up to that point it was only the absurdity of the position that had struck me. After that I began to get angry. (My daughter, by the way, goes to the PLC, Croydon. It occurs to me that these initials should now stand for Presbyterian Ladies Can't.)

Now I'm aware that in saying all this I am almost certainly preaching to the converted, and usually there is not much point in doing that except for the satisfaction of knowing that for once everyone agrees with you. But there are wider implications. Some of you must have wondered whether you can continue to belong to the Presbyterian Church. There is of course nothing wrong with a church containing a range of theological opinion: indeed the wider the range of opinion the stronger the church. So the fact that one disagrees with other people in the church doesn't mean that one has to leave. But where a church takes an official line which involves a contradiction of the essence of Christianity — as I think is the case here — then one has to consider one's position very seriously.

It would be wrong of me to tell you what you should do. It could for example be argued that the future of the Presbyterian Church would be better served by staying within the church and fighting this peculiar blend of obscurantism and uncharitableness. On the other hand, there are other considerations and other obligations, particularly to the young and to people outside the church. It seems to me that the Presbyterian Church is now in exactly the position of the Pharisees whom Jesus accused of shutting up the Kingdom of Heaven — they neither went in themselves nor did they allow others to enter. It is enough for me simply to bring the matter to your attention, and to make you aware that there are many within the Presbyterian Church who are asking themselves whether they should remain within it, and if so what they should do as a matter of urgency to change it.

Let me finish now with a slightly different argument. I said that one of the ostensible reasons behind the decision to ban the ordination of women was the passage in First Timothy. But there are probably other, more sinister reasons under the surface, such as fear, insecurity, puritanism and, above all I think, vanity — vanity based on a quite mistaken understanding of ordination. There are ministers who think that ordination is equivalent to a kind of rank which elevates them above ordinary sinners, gives them a unique access to God, and guarantees them a share in the life everlasting. They may not say so openly, but when they begin to close ranks and jealously guard their privileges, then one begins to question their motives and to suspect that they regard their ordination as a kind of shibboleth which opens the doors of the Kingdom of Heaven.

You may have seen in the newspaper towards the end of last year a report about a special women's language in China which has just been recovered by scholars. It had its origin in the oppression of women, it was their way of giving expression to their misery without fear of reprisal, because it was a language unintelligible to men. It seems as if these male ministers in the Presbyterian Church think the reverse: that they have a special way of saying things, a special language which is unintelligible to women, and which alone can catch the ear of the Almighty.

What I'm saying is this: it may be that the best argument against those who want to ban the ordination of women is not to ridicule their understanding of the Bible, nor to accuse them of insecurity or chauvinism or failure to move with the times, but simply to challenge their understanding of ordination. Ordination — being a minister — is not a privilege, nor does it attract any privileges. It doesn't mean that you're nearer to God, or more likely to go to heaven. (There is nothing self-contradictory about a minister going to hell.) Ordination doesn't make you different at all in the sight of God. It is merely a human act of appointing someone to preach and to administer the sacraments. The minister is simply a servant: he serves God and other people. One of the titles of the Pope is *servus servorum Dei*, a servant of the servants of God — and that applies to every minister.

And on that basis it seems to me, not that women should make as good ministers as men, but that they should make far better ministers. Women have the interests of others at heart far more naturally, far more instinctively, than men do. Men, I'm sorry to say, are essentially self-centred, aggressive, ambitious, assertive. Tenderness, kindness, patience are female virtues. If you think I'm being sentimental, read the New Testament and see how Jesus responded to the women he met, how he warmed to their maternal gentleness.

The really absurd thing about this questioning of the right of women to be ordained is not simply that it is unjustified, but that it is back to front. The question should be: what right have men to be ordained?

Imagination

$\mathcal{I}$ intend to be cynical this morning. The word cynic comes from the Greek word meaning 'a dog', and it goes back to a fellow called Diogenes in the fourth century BC, who decided to live like a dog. By that he meant rejecting all conventions — of religion, manners, dress, food, shelter. In fact he spent a large part of his life sitting in a tub, for reasons which are not entirely clear to me except that I suppose it was a cynical sort of thing to do. And he achieved such notoriety from his peculiar habits that even Alexander the Great went out of his way to visit him. Alexander found him sitting in his tub in the sun and asked him if there was anything he could do for him, to which Diogenes replied: 'Just get out of my light'.

Alexander was so impressed by this rudeness that he said to his attendants: 'If I were not Alexander I would choose to be Diogenes'. It is of course a question whether that option would have been available to him, because I think Alexander was somewhat deficient in that cynical quality which was so distinctive of Diogenes — that moral capacity to break out of the mould. Alexander followed exactly in his father's footsteps: indeed his adolescence was marred only by the fear that by the time he grew up his father might have made the job of conqueror redundant.

Diogenes on the other hand, though his name means 'born of Zeus the king of the gods', was in fact the son of a moneychanger who had served a term of imprisonment for defacing the coinage, and Diogenes used to say that he for his part was determined to deface the world's coinage — in other words to turn people's ideas upside down, and to show that what they regarded as important and valuable was in fact spurious. Openness of mind and moral courage are what cynicism in its original sense really involves.

One day last week, having an entirely open mind on what I should be preaching about this morning, I went into the Gillespie Library, which houses the College's theological collection. As always when I go into a theological library, I felt faintly depressed. There is something about the sight of all those endless shelves full of endless books about God that makes me lose hope before I begin. I often find myself wishing that, tucked away somewhere, just waiting to be discovered, there might be a little book, of no more than fifty pages, which had all the answers, so that it would be unnecessary ever to go to a library again.

But of course life is not like that. Some of you will remember the episode from *The Hitchhiker's Guide to the Galaxy* — that source of much wisdom through absurdity (rather like Diogenes) — when they found the biggest computer in the universe and asked it the question: 'What is the meaning of life?', and it churned away for about ten years and then spewed out the answer: 43. The point is of course that you can't have the answers in a vacuum. They depend on the question, and on the questioner; and the art of life I suppose lies in finding the right questions and having the courage to ask them.

At any rate, having failed to discover in the Gillespie Library any such slim volume with all the answers, I picked three books more or less at random, intending to dip into each and see if something suggested itself for this morning's sermon. That of course can be a dangerous thing to do. There is an old story about a man who applied this random method to the Bible, opening it anywhere with his eyes shut and placing his finger on what he hoped would be a verse with a special meaning for him. The first verse he picked out like this read: 'And Judas went out and hanged himself'. Not finding that very edifying he tried again, and this time he turned up the verse: 'Go thou and do likewise'. But my method wasn't quite as random as that. In fact what I extracted from each of the three books is connected in some way with the creation stories in the opening chapters of Genesis.

The first was a volume of St Thomas Aquinas, the greatest of the medieval theologians, who is still regarded by the Roman Catholic Church as the theologian par excellence, and who is known affectionately as the angelic doctor. The medieval theologians, or schoolmen as they were called, were celebrated for the sterility of their debates: for example about how many angels could dance on the point of a needle. (Certainly not many angelic doctors could, because Thomas Aquinas weighed in at around 110 kilos.) And it has to be said that to our modern minds there is a tendency to the absurd in Thomas's treatment of the creation stories, in his application of strict logic to the imaginative language of myth.

For example, he raises the question whether Adam and Eve would have made love in Paradise before the Fall, and he answers in the affirmative, on the grounds that God created man and woman before the Fall and can be presumed not to have given them any characteristics which would have remained superfluous if they had not fallen. Not only that; the Genesis story says that the woman was created in order to be a help to the man, and Thomas argues that this can only imply help in producing children since for any other purpose another man would have been much more useful.

But more interesting than this slightly wooden literalism is what the angelic doctor goes on to say, and that is that the pleasure Adam and Eve experienced from their love-making in Paradise must have been much greater than that after the Fall — on the basis that in Paradise their bodies and minds were purer.

What is remarkable about this is that St Thomas Aquinas could have had the open-mindedness and the moral courage to adopt such a position after a thousand years of repressive theology which had viewed sex as the result of the Fall, and therefore as something essentially depraved and greatly inferior to a state of celibacy. One thinks of Augustine, to whom the babe at its mother's breast was a symbol of concupiscence, and who found relief in the thought that there would be no sex in heaven. Thomas on the contrary not only saw sex as essentially good but maintained that it must have been even better in Paradise. Not surprisingly, these pages of his great work are seldom referred to.

The second book I took out of the library was by a modern Russian philosopher, Berdyaev, on the Destiny of Man. And it is interesting in itself that someone with as sophisticated and profound a mind as Berdyaev had should continue to find inspiration in the myths of the Garden of Eden. He concentrates on the tree of the knowledge of good and evil, and his question concerns the origin of good and evil: what was there before good and evil? After all, good and evil are correlatives, like light and darkness: the one implies the other. If there is no evil you can't talk about good. So what was there before Adam and Eve ate of the fruit of the tree? Paradise must have been a state before good and evil, and God must be on the other side of good and evil, beyond good and evil. It doesn't even make sense to call God good, because that is to judge God from the point of view of the good that has come into being after the Fall.

It's all very confusing, and one begins to wonder whether modern philosophers don't have too much in common with medieval theologians. But then Berdyaev says something much more arresting: that the true significance of God creating man in God's own image is that man is therefore also a creator. The Fall, Berdyaev says, was connected with freedom and this freedom, which of course we still have, involves a great deal more than simply the freedom to obey or disobey. According to Berdyaev, freedom really consists not in fulfilling the law but in creating new realities and new values which will ultimately lead beyond good and evil. 'Man', he says, 'is called not only to fulfil the good but to create it... Similarly in relation to God, man is free not merely in the sense that he can turn towards God or away from him... but in the sense of being able to co-operate with God, to create the good and produce new values'.

So, while Thomas Aquinas is in practice creative with the creation story, Berdyaev says that the creation story actually teaches the creativity of man. And this — apart from anything else — has profound implications for the status of the Bible: it is released from its fetters. Instead of being a dreary old statute-book which tells us, less and less convincingly, what we can and cannot do, it becomes both a charter of religious liberty and a challenge to join God in fashioning the future. Instead of being, as it tends to be in the hands of the Fundamentalists, a tyrannical oppressor with demonic overtones, the Bible becomes a living thing, speaking to our imaginations out of the imaginations of others, and therefore infinite in its possibilities.

And the third book I took out of the library is about exactly that: about the centrality of the imagination in theology and religion. It is by Professor John McIntyre, who was Principal of St Andrew's College in the 1950s. The book is a protest against too much conceptualising in theology, too much abstract thinking; and it is a plea for a greater use of the imagination, for thinking in images, as Jesus constantly does in his parables. For Professor McIntyre, the creation story is itself a description of God exercising his imagination, and so is the incarnation — in fact the idea of God becoming a man in order to lead men to God is the most imaginative idea conceivable. And our only hope, the only way in which we can be led to God, is through exercising our imaginations in return.

As an example of what I understand to be the exercise of this sort of imagination let me take the story of the Virgin Birth. There are two ways of looking at that story. First, you can insist on its literal truth. And if you do I have no objection at all. I just wonder whether, if it is literally true, it's really of much interest. The people I have spoken to who believe in the literal truth of the Virgin Birth have always seemed to be much more anxious to criticise those who don't agree with them, than to derive any comfort or theological significance from their belief. And it is an intriguing question why they believe in the literal truth of the Virgin Birth of Jesus and not in the very similar accounts from the ancient world about the birth of other famous figures — for example Alexander the Great, whose mother was said to have conceived by a serpent which was a god in disguise.

Now, such a story about Alexander the Great immediately suggests the other way of looking at the story of the Virgin Birth in the New Testament. It seems to me perfectly understandable that people should have been so impressed by Alexander's career that they found it necessary to invent and believe stories about the miraculous nature of his birth: it was an imaginative way of drawing attention to his greatness. It would not, however, be imaginative for us to insist that Alexander's father was actually a god disguised as a snake.

Similarly, a much more imaginative and therefore more profitable way of understanding the story of the Virgin Birth might be to say that it is rooted in contemporary reaction to the uniqueness of Jesus. That is that his contemporaries were so convinced that he reflected God, so to speak, and that he was in some sense different from any other human being that the only way they could adequately express this conviction was in terms of the fantastic. The story of the Virgin Birth, in other words, is a response of faith. It is not, according to this view, an *article* of faith implying that we have to respond in exactly the same way by believing it literally. What the story really requires of us is our own response, not so much to the story as to what inspired the story. It demands of us that we exercise our own imagination, and make our own — if possible — equally imaginative response to the person of Jesus.

What we really need, in fact, is a healthy dose of cynicism. Instead of going along on the same old tracks, like poor Alexander the Great — who ended up in tears because there were no more worlds to conquer — we should, like Diogenes, be turning the world upside down, and defacing the coinage, and telling the authorities, whoever they are, to get out of our light.

The Art of Life

THERE are forms of literature which most people read only at a certain stage in life. Poetry, for example. Most of us stop reading poetry, if we ever started, after the age of about twenty-five; and indeed very few people write poetry after that age. That may in fact be the distinguishing mark of poets, that they don't accept the ageing process, that they refuse to grow old — or to grow up. Belonging to the same class of what appeals to an essentially youthful readership are, I think, nineteenth century French and Russian novels. There is something sentimental and melancholic about them which strikes a chord in the late adolescent mind.

Certainly they struck a chord in me when I was about sixteen or seventeen. My father's bookshelves were full of these novels, unopened since he was young, and I would spend the long summer holidays reading books like *Sentimental Education* and *Crime and Punishment*. The questions they raised are now called existential questions: the great questions of life, which teenagers agonise over and strike attitudes over, and then a year or two later forget all about, sometimes forever. Questions like: What am I here for? Where am I going? What is the meaning of life?

And there was one book on those shelves which I remember particularly, though not for its contents. It was the title that grabbed my attention, and that is all I remember: the book was called *The Art of Life*. I've even forgotten the name of the author, though I know he was a Frenchman. The title astonished me, because it had never occurred to me that there could be such a thing as the art of life. For me, up to that point, life was simply something that happened to you; you took it as it came. In those days of highly disciplined boarding schools and authoritarian parents there was no question of being in control of life, of being captain of your destiny: you simply did what you were told was best for you. So the very idea of an art of life came as something of a release: I felt liberated by the mere possibility. And ever since then, I suppose, I've been trying to cultivate the art of life.

But the fact that I've forgotten everything about that book except its title is significant, because it is extremely difficult, if not impossible, to communicate the art of life, even supposing that one knows something about it. Because the art of life is not quite the same as the meaning of life, at least as that phrase is commonly understood. What I mean is that people talk about the meaning of life as if the answer could be given them in the form of an equation. 'What does it all mean?', they ask, when they're feeling down, and it's difficult to see what sort of answer could possibly satisfy them.

The point is that the art of life is not just a question of intellectual assent to propositions. Analogous is the relationship between religion and dogma: the more a church insists on the purity of its doctrine, the more endangered it is — it has lost its vitality, its reason for living. The true meaning of life can't be shared, it's not negotiable, you can only get at it by living yourself. And this applies even if the meaning of life turns out to be entirely negative. Socrates, for example, after a lifetime of struggling towards the meaning of life, was fond of saying: 'All I know is that I know nothing'. Now, as Kierkegaard pointed out, that's all very well coming from a hoary-headed sage, but if a schoolboy put down as an answer in an exam paper 'All I know is that I know nothing', he would justifiably be beaten for laziness or pretension, or both.

There is, in other words, no short cut to the meaning of life;

you have to get there, if at all, by living. And that is the question which is addressed by the art of life: how should life be lived so as to reach the meaning of life?

And it is this question which concerns most religious and ethical systems. I say most, because some think that the answer lies in turning your back on life — for example, religions which teach an escape from the world, or philosophies which advocate the avoidance of risks. Like the Stoics, who warned their followers against making any sort of human attachment: if you fell in love you risked being hurt, so the safest thing was not to fall in love. Happiness consisted in the absence of pain. If that were true, then the art of life would be to live as little as possible.

Now Christianity, as I understand it, is not like that. That is a fairly important qualification — 'as I understand it' — because of course there have been, and are, all sorts of interpretations of Christianity, some of which are distinctly life-denying. The Syriac Fathers, for example, didn't like women, or perhaps they liked them very much but thought it was wrong to like them, or perhaps they were afraid of them — psychologically there are several possibilities. And theologically they produced just as many reasons for their antipathy: for example, that Eve was responsible for all the woes of mankind, or that because Jesus was unmarried his followers should be too. But one of the Syriac Fathers, Aphraates, gives a reason very similar to that of the Stoics: he cites a character in the Old Testament who had two rebellious sons, and he says that this wouldn't have happened to him if he had remained celibate — therefore celibacy is a desirable state. And even in mainstream Christianity there is a pronounced streak of asceticism. For instance Paul says that it's better not to get married because the end of the world is at hand, and we should be thinking about that and not about how to please our wives.

But all this is a complete misunderstanding of the teaching of Jesus — as I understand it. There was nothing ascetic about Jesus. His enemies said of him that he was a glutton and a drunkard, and you can't convincingly spread rumours like that about an ascetic. And he had an extraordinary tenderness and sympathy for women, which comes over again and again. So, whatever he was, he wasn't life-denying. Indeed, in John's gospel he is quoted as saying: 'I came that you may have life, and have it abundantly'.

Now I'm not concerned here with whether Jesus in fact said that or, if he didn't, with what the writer of John's gospel meant by it. You may be interested to know that the consensus among modern scholars is that whoever said it, it wasn't Jesus; and whoever wrote it, it wasn't John. That is all irrelevant for my purposes because, whether Jesus said it or not, it strikes me as suggestive and profound; indeed as true. It may not be true that he said it, but what it says is true.

The question is: in what sense is it true that Jesus came in order that we might have life, and have it abundantly? How do we get at what Jesus's intentions were? There are of course various one-liners in the gospels, like the so-called Golden Rule: 'Whatever you wish that men would do to you, do so to them'. And there is a certain superficial attraction in reducing the whole of life to a single rule like this. It's like Kant's categorical imperative: always act so that the principle of your action could be made a universal law. Or it's like the story about a certain Jesuit, who was playing chess and drinking a pint of beer and minding his own business, when someone asked him what he would do if he were told that the world was to end in five minutes. He replied that he would go on playing chess and drinking beer — in other words his principle was that if a thing is morally justifiable at all the imminent end of the world has nothing to do with it.

But the trouble with all these universal rules or principles is simply this: that you can't sum up the whole of life in a single sentence. You have to be shown how to live, not just told. So the sayings of Jesus have to be filled out against the background of his lifestyle, and set off against the rest of his teaching. And when you do that you find, I think, broadly speaking, two strands on the subject of the art of life. The difficulty is that on the face of it they contradict each other.

The first is illustrated in this passage from the Sermon on the Mount: 'Do not be anxious about your life, what you shall eat or what you shall drink, nor about your body, what you shall put on... Do not be anxious about tomorrow... Let the day's own trouble be sufficient for the day'. In other words, live in the present, or as Horace put it: *carpe diem*, improve the shining hour.

And this is very good advice, because one of the depressing things about growing old — and by old I mean about twenty-five onwards — is that you lose the capacity to respond to the immediacy of the present. Your life becomes controlled by ambition, career prospects, promotion and, at the end of it all, that twentieth century reinterpretation of heaven or hell: the size of your superannuation.

So it's a crucial aspect of the art of life, this concentration on the present. But of course by itself it's suspect, it's open to abuse, it can easily degenerate into the attitude 'eat, drink and be merry, for tomorrow we die'. It's a recipe for complacency and stagnation. There has to be an antidote.

And the antidote is to be found in another dimension of Jesus's teaching and lifestyle. You find it in sayings like 'Take up your cross and follow me', or 'Leave the dead to bury their dead', or 'He who loses his soul for my sake will find it'. And you find it in Jesus's nomadic, peripatetic way of life, and in his final decision to lay down his life. In other words, this is the future dimension, which is prepared to jettison the present and all its attractions and ties; which is always ready to sacrifice at the drop of a hat.

But to concentrate solely on the future is equally one-sided and equally suspect — and equally open to abuse. Some of the early Christians positively courted martyrdom, and made it clear that life wasn't worth living unless they could end up being thrown to the lions. And some of the medieval saints actually wallowed in discomfort, licking the suppurating sores of beggars and so on, in a grotesque attempt to enter the Kingdom of Heaven.

And the church generally is always tempted to put too much emphasis on the future and to turn its back on the reality of the present. This shows itself in a kind of religious masochism which says that if you're enjoying yourself it must be wrong. It also shows itself in the attitude which accepts all sorts of present misery — usually involving other people — on the grounds that some future paradise will more than compensate. But as Dostoevsky said, if God expected him to ignore the sufferings of one little girl simply by offering him a place in heaven then he would respectfully return his entrance ticket.

So the art of life, in Christian terms, cannot consist either in turning your back on the future and seizing the passing moment or in turning your back on the present and losing your soul in order to find it. Either by itself is incomplete and inadequate.

But how are the two to be reconciled, or held together? Again, this is not the sort of question you can expect to be answered by some neat formula. It's the sort of question Jesus would have answered by means of a parable, so I shall try to do the same. There is an old Russian fable about a peasant who saved all his life in order to go on a pilgrimage to Jerusalem. At last, when he was an old man of about seventy, he had got together the hundred roubles necessary for the trip and the whole village gave him a special send-off. It was the fulfilment of his life's dream; everything he had ever done had been leading up to this. The next day he was back. He had met a sick beggar by the roadside and had been so troubled by the beggar's condition that he had given him the hundred roubles.

Now that peasant had spent his entire life living for the future, always denying himself and working towards the ultimate pilgrimage. But then suddenly, in a complete reversal, the whole purpose of his life was thrown overboard, the future abandoned to a whim, everything concentrated on the present instant. His action was on the face of it absurd, paradoxical — and, I think, intensely Christian.

In other words, the art of life consists in holding these two contradictory principles in tension. Live in the present, yes: but always under the shadow of the future. Always be prepared to jettison the present in favour of the future; seize the day by the scruff of the neck but never let it control you, never let it get *you* by the scruff, never forget your dream of the far-off Jerusalem. And conversely, aim for the future, yes: but never so completely at the expense of the present that you fail to see reality under your nose, as that peasant would have done if he had pressed on to Jerusalem and ignored the beggar at the roadside. Never turn your back on life.

Matriculation

$\mathcal{I}$ want to begin by giving you two brief glimpses into my social life over the past few weeks. The first involved a cocktail party for various university people. At a late stage I found myself with a professor of some scientific discipline, I forget what exactly, although he told me about it at great length. I remember something about genetic engineering, but that's all. At any rate, having eventually exhausted himself, he asked without much interest what I did. When I said I was a theologian he looked at me with undisguised dismay and said: 'You don't honestly believe all that rubbish, do you?'

I suppose that it was a compliment in one way. It implied that my conversation up to that point had given the impression that I was reasonably normal; on the other hand, the further implication was that this impression must have been false, and that if I were really a theologian then I must in fact be some kind of idiot.

Then the other day I was at a lunch party, and people were talking about the heat and light in Australia. I said facetiously that of course coming from Scotland I was accustomed to living in the dark; whereupon the woman sitting next to me said that this was a very peculiar thing for a minister of religion to say, because she would have expected me to exist in a permanent state of enlightenment. I laughed politely, and then realised that she was deadly serious.

I mention these two trivial incidents because they represent very common perceptions of the status and content of religion, and specifically of Christianity in the late twentieth century. I imagine that most of you who are matriculating today, coming into this chapel for the first and possibly the second last time (I should remind you that the Valedictory Service when you leave College is also compulsory) — most of you must have felt that you were entering a world which has nothing whatever to do with sober reason and the kind of disciplined scientific intellectual processes to which you are accustomed, or at least hope to become accustomed. And you may also have thought that you were about to be exposed to the kind of otherworldly religious brightness which is so remote from normal experience that it succeeds only in blinding outsiders.

I would like therefore to try to refute both of the suggestions implicit in my two social encounters: the suggestion that Christianity is a question of having to believe rubbish; and the suggestion that it necessarily involves some kind of enlightenment.

First, believing rubbish. Well of course it is probably true that most religious people do believe a certain amount of rubbish. It is probably true that everybody believes a certain amount of rubbish, even your most scientific of thinkers. For example, my professor of science showed that he himself was guilty of believing rubbish, in uncritically accepting that all theologians necessarily believed rubbish. We all have a certain number of untested assumptions about each other and about the world we live in, which if we were more careful or more honest we would recognise to be absurd.

But I would want to go much further than that, and question whether Christianity is really about believing anything at all. Of course that sort of remark, unqualified, can be simply irritating: it's the sort of thing trendy clerics say, to grab attention. Those of you who are familiar with *Yes, Minister*, will remember Sir Humphrey's definition of theology: 'Theology is the device which enables agnostics to remain within the church'. But I think it may be true that we have reached the point where Christian agnosticism is not only attractive but necessary.

There is a very old distinction which theologians operate

with, and which is expressed rather neatly in Latin: it is the distinction between the *fides quae creditur* and the *fides qua creditur* — between the faith which is believed, and the faith by which we believe. In other words there is a difference between, on the one hand, Christianity as a series of propositions or credal statements, like 'I believe in the Virgin Birth', and, on the other hand, Christianity as some sort of relationship. It is not of course an absolute distinction, because properly speaking the propositions are intended simply to express more fully the nature of the relationship and, conversely, the relationship itself has an inevitable tendency both to generate propositions and to feed on them. But it is a difference of emphasis and of attitude which has always been apparent in Christianity, and it is more obvious now than ever.

One kind of religious temperament, which at its extreme results in Fundamentalism, insists on the content above all else. Christianity, according to this view, is a series of propositions, largely contained in the Bible, and the chief proposition outside the Bible is that the Bible itself is infallible and inerrant. The Bible for the Fundamentalist is a statute-book which lays down everything necessary for the Christian life. The rest is simply obedience. This is the *fides quae creditur*, the faith which is believed, carried to the limit. And it doesn't matter what sort of nonsense results, or what sort of unkindness or even cruelty. If the Bible says that women are subordinate, then women will remain subordinate. Indeed the Fundamentalist is quite impervious to argument. If you say to him that he is talking rubbish he will be indifferent: if the Bible tells him to talk rubbish, then talk rubbish he will. There was an early Church Father named Tertullian who expressed very succinctly how impregnable this position can be. When someone accused him of believing rubbish he replied, *Credo quia absurdum*: I believe it, because it's rubbish.

I think that my friend the Scientific Professor probably had people like Tertullian or the modern Fundamentalists in mind. And if so I sympathise. But what I'm saying is that there is another dimension to Christianity, another conception of what faith means, the *fides qua creditur*, the faith by which you believe, the attitude to life which sustains you.

Now I don't mean that, rather than being a case of millions

of Fundamentalists all quoting the Bible at each other, Christianity should become instead a case of millions of mystics all on their knees in separate communion with God. This is where my other social encounter comes into play — the woman who thought I should be a permanent example of religious enlightenment. My first proposition is that Christianity should not be a matter of propositions, it should be a religion without content. My second proposition is that Christianity is not a matter of enlightenment, but of enabling us to live in the dark.

And of course the two perspectives are related. The Fundamentalist peddles certainty, even if his certainties are absurd. That is why his wares are so attractive; that is why Fundamentalism is so widespread, not just in the Presbyterian Church of Australia and not just in Christianity: it is one of the most extraordinary expansions of the late twentieth century. But really there is nothing so extraordinary about it. We live in an age of unprecedented uncertainty, largely because we have unprecedented freedom — freedom both to think and to act. Freedom brings uncertainty, and uncertainty breeds fear — fear of freedom. The perfect antidote to freedom is rules, rules to obey. People don't want freedom, they want to be told what to do. So Fundamentalism has a field day, and so Christianity is portrayed and perceived as a religion of propositions, assent to which and obedience to which will produce enlightenment.

I think this is unfortunate. It may of course succeed in bringing happiness and security to many people. But it is a questionable happiness: it is the happiness of the old lag who feels safe locked up in his cell, away from the confusion and responsibility of the outside world. And to many more people in the outside world Christianity is presented as a religion which is intellectually and morally bankrupt.

And this means that Fundamentalism is not only unfortunate but demonic. I may not believe in demons, but I do believe in the demonic, in the sense of a sinister distortion of the essence of Christianity. Because the god whom the Fundamentalist believes in, reflected in his attitude to the Bible, is an authoritarian god, a statute-giver, a god who commands and who expects obedience. And, ironically enough, that is precisely the misconception of God which Jesus spent his life trying to undermine.

God, according to Jesus, isn't in the least interested in rules or obedience. Nor is he in the least authoritarian. Nor does he expect us to believe rubbish. Nor does he offer enlightenment. In fact, by the standards of some other religions, and by the standards of the Fundamentalists, he's not much of a God at all. One could easily overlook him completely.

Indeed, properly speaking there is nothing miraculous about Christianity; at least nothing miraculous in any sensational way. Because what Jesus offered, what Christianity offers, is simply the capacity to face up to reality without having to believe in rubbish; and to live in the dark, to put up with uncertainty, without having to sacrifice our freedom. How it does that, I can't tell you — I mean I can't even tell you more precisely what it involves. Because that can only be your own private story, each one of you individually. And it may not be the time yet even for the beginning of that story — it may be a long way off. All I want to say today is: don't dismiss Christianity, don't dismiss the idea of God, don't listen to professors of science or of anything else who assume that it's all rubbish, and don't listen to society ladies who assume that it's all sweetness and light.

Valedictory

THERE is a story about a famous professor of philosophy in the University of Oxford at the beginning of this century, who used to address his first year students in these words: 'Gentlemen', he would say, 'you are now about to embark on a course of studies which will occupy you for three years. Together they form a noble adventure. But I would like to remind you of an important point. When you go down from the University, you will go into the church, or to the bar, or to parliament, or into the army, or into industry or commerce, or into various other professions. Let me make this clear to you: nothing you will learn in the course of your studies here will be of the slightest possible use to you in later life, save only in this: that if you work hard and intelligently, you should be able to detect when a man is talking rubbish — and that is the main purpose of education'.

That story seems appropriate to a Valedictory Service: I imagine that many of you are wondering just what it is you have learnt in the last three or four years. Those of you, that is, who are like Manning Clark, who spent his whole time at Melbourne University haunted by the feeling that there must be some other course in the syllabus in which one learnt the important things. He never found it, and indeed went through life hoping that one day someone would tell him what it was all about.

I had a somewhat similar experience myself in my first year at university, though considerably more concentrated. In fact it was on my first day in the Law Faculty at Edinburgh University, at my very first lecture. I had no idea really what to expect from the law — I had what you might call an open mind — so I wasn't very surprised, as I sat at the back of the lecture hall with an old school friend, that I didn't understand a word of what the lecturer was saying. My friend and I must have had roughly the same intelligence quotient because it dawned on us both simultaneously, after a good half hour of bewilderment and only when the lecturer began writing a mathematical formula on the board, that we were in the wrong place entirely and had been listening to the opening lecture on first year Physics.

The point of all this, the lesson from the story of the philosophy professor and from Manning Clark and from my own humiliating experience, is that what you learn in your time at university, if anything, is unlikely to be learnt in the lecture room. I'm thinking not of practical skills or factual information but of the valuable things: like intellectual honesty, courage, loyalty, sincerity and what has been called ultimate concern — a consuming interest in what life is all about. There are no university courses in any of these things, nor could there be, but without them every subject is deficient, and without them no one can be considered properly educated.

It may be, however, that this is where the Colleges come into their own. And it may well be what the founding fathers of this College had in mind when they declared that one of the main purposes of the College was to provide its residents with what they called systematic religious education.

Of course that expression, which is still enshrined in the College's Incorporation Act, is somewhat daunting and archaic, and that probably accounts for the fact that it seems nowadays to be more honoured in the breach than in the observance. So I shall proceed to rectify that now by giving you some religious education. It can scarcely be called systematic, but on the basis that everyone comes to chapel at the beginning of their first year and at the end of their last year it is at least regular.

Now when I say that I am going to give you some religious education, what I mean is that I want to tell you what I think religion really is, and how it is connected with those valuable things I spoke about, like honesty, sincerity, ultimate concern and so on. As usual, it is easier to begin by saying what in my opinion religion is not. It is not an obsession with the after-life. It is often taken to be that: for example the apostle Paul says somewhere that 'If for this life only we have hoped in Christ, we are of all men most to be pitied'. So you get the tradition of morbid martyrs, falling over themselves to get into the Kingdom of Heaven — people like Ignatius, who thought his life would have been a complete waste if he didn't end up being thrown to the lions. This is the life-denying interpretation of Christianity, according to which you live only really in order to die.

And you find the same thing in other religions. For example, in China in the second century BC people were convinced that the land of immortality existed somewhere in the west, the Islands of the Blest they called it, and one of the great emperors used to send fleets of ships every year, containing thousands of young men and maidens, to find these Islands of the Blest. Whatever they found on their voyages, these young men and maidens, they never came back, and the Emperor spent most of his life sitting disconsolately at the edge of the sea, dreaming of eternity. Indeed, in a fine irony, one of the commonest causes of death among educated Chinese at a certain period was overdosing on elixirs of immortality: a kind of Eastern equivalent of the Faust story, and much more succinct.

But this is a one-sided and unfortunate interpretation of religion, and I think myself that Paul's remark should be reversed: 'If for immortality only we have hoped in Christ, then of all men we are most to be pitied'. Religion I think is very much a matter for this life and this world, and specifically it is really concerned with the critical moments of your life and with how you react at these critical moments. I don't mean at all that it has no bearing on everyday life: I mean that people's true spirit is shown not in how they treat their family, or in how much they give to their local church, or in how pious they are. I have suffered enough from holy people in my time not to be taken in by piety. And I remember an old lady I knew when I was a minister, who was the daughter of a famous divinity professor and whose favourite saying was: 'Heaven preserve us from holy women'.

Religion is not a matter of being holy, but of the decisions you make in life. I took a service the other day in a church on the North Shore, and afterwards I was introduced to a very fierce lady. It was a hot day, but she was wearing a tweed suit and a very angry expression. She was not a holy woman; she belonged in fact to the species which I call angry Christians. She told me that she was writing a book — or, as she modestly put it, another book — on Japanese Christianity, or Christianity in Japan; and she said, referring to some massacre in the eighteenth century, 'persecution of course soon gets rid of the rubbish'. I thought at the time that this was a little uncharitable, and perhaps lacking in compassion to those of us who are made of less stern stuff, but on reflection I realised that of course she was right. Christianity, religion, is not a matter of being good, or kind, or pious, any more than life is about what you learn in the lecture hall. It is a matter of courage, honesty, sincerity, taking risks, making impossible decisions, doing what the world thinks is absurd.

Now at this point I was going to give you three examples of what I mean, in the interests of being systematic, but I've decided to exercise compassion. My reason is that when I was back in Scotland last month someone reminded me of something my daughter said when she was about two years old, shortly after I became a minister. It was in church. I was well launched into my sermon and had reached perhaps the third point, when my daughter suddenly got up from the front row and said in a loud voice: 'That's enough: home now!'

So I'll give you just one example. It's the well-known example of Martin Luther at the Diet of Worms in 1521. Luther in his own field was a genius, in the same sense that Napoleon was a genius in his: they both had that extraordinary gift for cutting through irrelevancies and getting straight to the heart of the problem — the genius of simplicity. As well as that Luther was a brilliant scholar and linguist, a man of immense theological learning. And for years he had lived the ascetic life of a monk, struggling to subdue his natural appetites. But none of that to my mind makes him particularly interesting: the world is full of scholars, and ascetics, and even genius is not so scarce. What really sets him apart is the scene at the Diet of Worms.

He has been summoned before the Holy Roman Emperor to answer a charge of heresy. And it is important to understand exactly what is involved in this in the early sixteenth century. It's not just a matter of life and death, even if that sounds a bit Irish — there are worse things than death. In the sixteenth century, to be accused of heresy and found guilty means that the entire civilised world is against you, religious and secular. You are treated as an outcast, as dirt; everywhere there is hostility and anger and scorn and derision. You are an upstart, with the gall to think that you alone are in a position to put right 1500 years of history. And, worse than all that, there is the thought at the back of your mind that perhaps you are wrong, and that therefore God also is against you.

So it's not surprising that Luther, being human, wavers. At his first appearance before the Emperor he is confronted with a pile of his own books and asked if he acknowledges them. He does, in a whisper. He is then asked whether he still wants to defend everything in them, or whether he disowns any part of them. To the astonishment of the Emperor, and of everyone else, and indeed of every historian since then, Luther asks for time to think it over. If the fierce lady in the tweed suit had seen him then, she would no doubt have dismissed him as rubbish.

But the next day things are different. He is asked the same question, and this time there is no hesitation. He makes a long and passionate speech in his own defence, at the end of which he says: 'I cannot and I will not recant anything, for to go against conscience is neither right nor safe. *Hier stehe ich, ich kann nicht anders*'. Here I stand: I have no choice.

That, in a nutshell, is what religion is. It is not something that you learn in lectures. You might catch a glimpse of it in certain people, or on the sports field; but essentially it is a seed which is planted in you, a divine spark, whose presence you may be unaware of until the time comes for you to make use of it. It is enough if you are aware of its possibility: that is all you can do, and that is all you have to do. When the time comes, you will find yourself acting as it were in spite of yourself. But if you deny the possibility, if you exclude the divine, then you may be happy, you may be prosperous, you may be famous — but you will never do anything worthwhile.

Roots

*L*AST Saturday I was given a ticket to the Australia-Scotland rugby match at the Sydney Football Ground. I thought that, having lived in Australia for eighteen months, it was going to be an interesting test of where my loyalties lay, but in the end there was no doubt. Scotland were soundly beaten, and I was thoroughly dejected. In fact I would really rather not have gone at all, because for the first time since we came to Australia I felt the pangs of homesickness. I had a very good seat, very near the action, and seeing these familiar faces, which I had last seen at Murrayfield in Edinburgh, brought back all the atmosphere of the internationals which I began watching with my father when I was about ten years old. I thought about the state of Scottish rugby then and now, and came to the conclusion that things hadn't changed much. The distinctive thing about the Scots is not that they win more than anyone else, but that they're the best losers in the world — they never give up, they always go down fighting, they're never less than lion-hearted.

And then I asked myself why that is the case: why is there that kind of continuity in a team? Well partly, I suppose, it's something that's handed down from father to son. My father passed on to me his feelings about Scottish rugby, just as his father had influenced him thirty years before. And it's an extraordinary thought, how this contact between father and son can make history telescope. Someone calculated that if you allow about twenty-five years on average between generations, you need only eighty fathers and sons to get back to the days of Jesus; only a hundred and twenty to get back to King David; and the front ten rows of this church filled with fathers and sons would take you back to the time of Moses.

But of course that is an artificial way of looking at it, and grossly oversimplified. History doesn't work like that; in reality everything is mixed up and blurred and overlapping. And that in fact is where the secret of this continuity lies: the Scottish rugby team has never been completely new since it was formed over a hundred years ago. There has always been a nucleus inherited from the previous year. Each year there are on average perhaps four or five new players, and the rest are old hands. So that some of the team I saw on Saturday had played with the great names of five or ten years ago, and they in turn had played with the stars of the seventies, and so on back to the teams I used to watch as a boy, and to the teams my father used to watch. And that accounts, I think, for the amazing sense of loyalty both in the team and in the supporters, a sense of corporateness, of belonging. It's not just chauvinism, or mindless nationalism, as it would be if a new sport were invented and Scotland fielded a team from scratch. There would be none of the same emotion, nothing of that almost mystical identification with the past.

Now all this is very similar to the idea of apostolic succession, which some of the early church fathers used to refute their heretical opponents. They argued, these early fathers, that the historical link between the contemporary bishops and their predecessors — going right back to the apostles — was the guarantee of their orthodoxy, of the correctness of their beliefs. Of course, applied too narrowly this can be a two-edged weapon: what happens when you get a heretical bishop? But there is undoubtedly a profound spiritual truth in the idea. And like most spiritual truths, it is not really susceptible of rational explanation: it is something you feel — like the atmosphere at Murrayfield.

Take the hymn we're going to sing at the end of this service: 'O God of Bethel, by whose hand thy people still are fed, who through this weary pilgrimage hast all our fathers led'. It's one of the most moving hymns in the hymn-book; partly, I'm sure, because it was the hymn which was always sung by the Scottish emigrants to New Zealand and Australia in the nineteenth century, when their ships set sail and they looked back at the land they would never see again. The strange thing is, I don't think you need to know this to be moved by the hymn. It's as if the words and the tune have acquired an emotional flavour which has been handed down through the generations ever since, and which is now inseparably attached.

Many of these Scottish emigrants were the victims of the Highland clearances: they had been evicted, often brutally, from their crofts by landlords who wanted a better return for their money, and who replaced them with sheep. My own great-grandfather was one of these victims. His earliest memory, apparently, was of sitting on his mother's knee as a little boy of about five, while their croft was burnt to the ground beside them and she wept inconsolably. When I was a little boy my parents took me to the site of that croft, and something about the atmosphere of the place, the desolate glen and the heather and the mist, made me burst into tears too. And I'm sure it wasn't just auto-suggestion or sentimentality: it has remained one of my own earliest memories, and I think there was something atavistic about it, as if I was somehow in touch with what had happened, as if it were a family memory implanted in me from birth and independent of knowledge or experience. That kind of feeling is deeper than anything; it is in the fabric of our make-up, it is part of us. And it's that kind of shiver many of us get when we sing these lines: 'God of our fathers! Be the God of their succeeding race'.

But of course there is another aspect to this. Our connections with the past, with our ancestors, are not simply romantic: they involve obligations, responsibilities as well. That is perhaps not the best way of putting it, because it sounds rather as if people who have these feelings have to be reminded of their duties. Usually they don't. Usually, indeed, they are likely to react with passionate indignation if any part of their inheritance is in the least threatened.

Look for example at the way Paul reacts in his letter to the Galatians to the threat represented by his opponents there. He is under attack and he comes out fighting. Indeed he says some very extreme, not to say inflammatory, things. 'I'm appalled', he says to the Galatians, 'at the way you've been behaving... You gullible Galatians, you've been indoctrinated'. Then with a dreadful pun he says of his circumcising opponents that he wishes they would castrate themselves.

Now it was in fact this insistence by his opponents on circumcision which provoked all this passion. And it is easy for us to dismiss the whole issue as irrelevant to our contemporary scene. What has the primitive rite of circumcision to do with us? But behind it lies an issue of principle which is still very much alive. Circumcision was symbolic in this context of the status of the Law, which really meant the Old Testament and what it revealed of God's will. To the Jews of the first century the Law was God's supreme gift to Israel, and man's response to God was measured by his obedience to the Law. The Law was the ultimate and universal yardstick.

And because the Law said that circumcision was an essential step in becoming one of God's people, the Judaizers among the Galatians were insisting that to become a Christian you had to be circumcised. In other words, they put the Law above Christ: you could only come to Christ through the channels laid down by the Law. But for Paul the Law had ceased to be the supreme standard. Instead he measured everything by his experience of Christ. And the death and resurrection of Christ indicated to him that circumcision was irrelevant: the gospel was for everyone and no one had to qualify, or indeed could qualify. To Paul this controversy about the necessity for circumcision was a matter of life and death — the whole of Christianity depended on the outcome. And if it hadn't been for the stand that Paul took, we wouldn't be here today: Christianity would have remained a sect of Judaism.

And a very similar situation faces many churches today, among them the Presbyterian Church of Australia, because we are confronted today by an attitude to the Bible which is in many respects analogous to the way in which Paul's opponents in Galatia viewed the Law. It is an attitude which treats the Bible as a kind of statute-book, to which Christians owe blind and unquestioning obedience, even if the results are absurd or — what is worse — uncharitable. It is in fact the attitude of the Fundamentalists, although they prefer to be known by euphemisms like conservative or reformed evangelicals.

And just as the Judaizers in the Galatian churches put the Law above Christ, so the Fundamentalists are in danger of putting the Bible above Christ. The danger is epitomised in the story about an old lady in the north of Scotland a century ago, who was a very determined Christian and a staunch sabbatarian. When someone attempted to point out to this lady that Jesus himself had broken the rules of the Sabbath, she replied: 'Aye, I know, and I've never thought ony the better o' him for it'.

I'll give you another example of this kind of blinkered attitude from ecclesiastical history. St Augustine at the beginning of the fifth century devoted several years of his life to combating the party of the Donatists. The Donatists saw the church as a community of saints, a kind of Noah's Ark full of pure Christians sailing over the defiling waters of the world, but protected from them by a thick coat of pitch inside and out. It was a church on the defensive, intent only on preserving its identity. For Augustine this was behaving just like the old Israel, putting static obedience to rules above everything else. And it represented a major threat to the future of the church. Because for Augustine the church symbolised God's purpose in the world; indeed it stood poised to take over the whole world. He summed up the Donatists' attitude in these words: 'The clouds roll with thunder, that the House of the Lord should be built throughout the earth: and these frogs sit in their marsh and croak: "We are the only Christians!"'

And that is precisely what the Fundamentalists say. 'We are the only Christians', they say, and they shout 'Heresy!' whenever anyone disagrees with them. And they are hijacking the church, by insisting that this is the only possible way of looking at things.

But of course there are other ways of looking at the Bible. Certainly the Bible is the word of God — but only if it is a living, dynamic thing, which is constantly being reinterpreted and reassessed by each new generation. Certainly the Bible is inspired — but not in a wooden, literalistic way. It is a collection of inspired insights into the nature of God, but that doesn't mean that every part is equally inspired; or that one cannot treat parts of it as time-bound, or even as sub-Christian and mistaken — for example, notoriously, Paul's attitude to women in the church.

Now this threat, the threat represented by a Fundamentalist approach to the Bible, is the greatest threat your Presbyterian Church of Australia has faced since its inception. It may of course survive, even if the Fundamentalists do take over completely. It may even still be called the Presbyterian Church. But it will cease to have any connection with the church of your fathers. The Presbyterian tradition your church has inherited has nothing to do with Fundamentalism, or obscurantism, or bigotry, or intolerance. On the contrary, it is a tradition which involves on the one hand a highly educated ministry — broadminded, receptive to new ideas, adventurous, and above all rigorously honest; and on the other hand a fiercely independent laity — decent, charitable, fair, and above all willing to use their minds and to speak their minds. Entirely foreign to your tradition is any suggestion of indoctrination, or manipulation, or bully-boy tactics.

But for the first time you are in danger of finding yourselves with a completely new team, bearing no relation to the teams of your fathers, and having nothing in common with them. You owe it to your church, you owe it to your fathers, to fight for the principles they believed in, so that you can sing without any reservation: 'God of our fathers, be the God of their succeeding race!'

The Watchman

$\mathcal{G}$OD said to Ezekiel: 'I have made you a watchman for the house of Israel'. (Ezekiel 33:7.)

This is one of the great dramatic images in the Old Testament. It's an image which has lost some of its force for us, because most of us don't have much to do directly with nuclear early warning systems, which I suppose are our modern equivalent of the watchman. But in ancient Israel each walled city had its watchman, whose duty it was to look out for the approach of an enemy, and then to blow a blast on his trumpet. Then everyone working in the fields or the vineyards outside the city would at once seek refuge behind the walls. If they didn't, if they weren't listening, or if they thought it was a false alarm and didn't bother to go back to the city, then their blood would be upon their own heads. But if the watchman saw the enemy coming and failed to blow the trumpet, then he would be personally responsible for all the bloodshed that ensued.

Now, says God to Ezekiel, your responsibility as a prophet is of that magnitude. If you fail to warn the wicked man, if you fail to pass on the message that I give you, then you and the wicked man are equally responsible and you will both die.

It's an image which underlies both the urgency of the prophet's task and his accountability to God and to his fellows. But like all potent ideas in the sphere of religion it is susceptible to distortion and perversion. And in the history of Christianity the role of the believer, or of the church, as a watchman frequently has been distorted and perverted. I mention just two examples.

First, the Inquisition in the sixteenth century. The Inquisitors were driven by a great zeal for the salvation of others: so much so that they were prepared to kill the body in order to save the soul. They argued that heresy was the greatest of all crimes, because it was an insult to God, the greatest of beings. It was worse than treason, for example, because it was directed against a heavenly king; it was worse than counterfeiting money, because it counterfeited the truth of salvation. Therefore the penalty attached to it could not be less than the penalties for treason or counterfeiting. The penalty the Inquisitors chose was burning at the stake: they avoided beheading because 'the Church abhors bloodshed'. And they persuaded themselves that all their terrible cruelty was necessary and justifiable and was motivated by love — love for the victim's soul. They used Augustine's analogy of saving the body by amputating the limb, and they saw the heretic as the rotten limb and the church as the body. And in their role as watchmen protecting the city of God from the enemy in the shape of heretics, they developed an extraordinary and terrifying apparatus of secret police, spies, informers, interrogators and torture. All out of love for the body of Christ and for the soul of the heretic.

My second example of how the office of watchman has been perverted comes from my own country, Scotland, in the period after the Reformation, when the Kirk Sessions tried to exercise what they called Godly Discipline. They wielded enormous power. Anyone whom they excommunicated automatically became a kind of outlaw from the state: excommunicated persons were incapable of holding office, of giving evidence at law, of holding lands or rents. And the social effects of being brought to public repentance in sackcloth could be devastating. The terror and shame which some unmarried mothers felt at the prospect of being paraded before the congregation drove them to kill their babies.

And of course where there is power there are informers — an informer is a kind of self-appointed watchman — and there was plenty of scope for them. The records of the Kirk Sessions of the period are filled with references to the crimes of fornication, adultery, blasphemy, sabbath-breaking, slander, drunkenness, swearing, unnatural offences and witchcraft. And those accused of witchcraft were often tortured horribly before they confessed. In 1596 a woman eventually, and not surprisingly, confessed to being a witch after she had been kept for 48 hours in the cashielaws, which were a kind of iron case for the leg to which fire was gradually applied. Her family were tortured in front of her: her husband in the long irons, her son in the iron boots, and her daughter in the pilniewinks, which crushed the fingers. And all in the name of the Father, and of the Son, and of the Holy Spirit.

Now not only did the Kirk Sessions' interpretation of their role as watchman result in lovelessness and cruelty and an intolerable invasion of privacy, it also had the side effect of equating sin with sex in the popular mind. The great majority of the sins, or crimes as they called them, which the Kirk Sessions devoted their energies to rooting out, were sexual in nature: probably because they were most easily identified. It was much easier to produce in evidence an illegitimate baby than it was to point to the fruits of pride, or greed, or self-righteousness, or hypocrisy. This emphasis on sexual immorality as the heart of sin, as the root of all evil, was quite without foundation in the Bible, but it became widespread in Scotland and it has not altogether died out even now.

Well, we see how easily the image of the watchman lends itself to that kind of perversion of its original purpose. But so that we can see just where the Inquisitors and the Kirk Sessions went wrong let me give you two examples of watchmen in the proper sense, two men who saw their function not as arbiters of morality or religious belief, not as interfering oppressors, but as liberators from mistaken understandings of God's nature.

First, a young man who taught in St Andrews in Scotland shortly before the Reformation — Patrick Hamilton. Hamilton had studied in Paris and become familiar there with Luther's doctrines. When these were outlawed in Scotland he continued to speak out in favour of them, and soon he was accused of heresy and fled the country. He went to Germany and met Luther, and at the newly founded University of Marburg he wrote a famous book which a contemporary said contained the pith of all divinity. But that wasn't enough for him. Though he had been driven from home by the accusation of heresy, a year later he returned to St Andrews and taught Luther's doctrines and disputed openly in the University. He was left at liberty for a month: the establishment probably hoped he would have the sense to go away again so that they wouldn't have to act. But he forced their hand: as Peter said in the Book of Acts, he could not but speak of what he had seen and heard. At last he was arrested, tried and condemned. On 29 February 1528 he was burned at the stake in St Andrews, the first Scottish martyr. His last distinct words were these: 'Lord Jesus, receive my spirit. How long shall darkness overwhelm this realm? And how long wilt thou suffer this tyranny of men?'

Patrick Hamilton saw himself as a watchman appointed by God, he felt constrained to speak out in favour of Luther's teaching; he thought that if he took the easy way out and stayed away from Scotland and closed his mouth, then he would be in the position of the watchman who sees the enemy approaching and does nothing. And he was prepared to die rather than do nothing.

The second example was not only prepared to die: he was prepared to kill. Dietrich Bonhoeffer, a German pastor and one of the most adventurous theological minds of this century, was hanged by the Nazis in 1945 for his part in the conspiracy to assassinate Hitler. You can imagine the mental torment a minister of religion must have gone through in arriving at such an interpretation of his duty. But who will say that he was wrong? That was no time for sitting on the fence. And the alternative was to condone what Hitler was doing. Here is an extract from a German church magazine reporting the failure of the attempt on Hitler's life, which puts that alternative point of view:

> The frightful day. While our brave armies, courageous unto death, are struggling manfully to protect their country and to achieve final victory, a handful of infamous officers, driven by their own ambition, ventured on a frightful crime and made an attempt to murder the Fuhrer. The Fuhrer was

saved and this unspeakable disaster averted from our people. For this we give thanks to God with all our hearts, and pray, with all our church congregations, for God's assistance and help in the grave tasks that the Fuhrer has to perform in these most difficult times.

I emphasise, this was a church magazine.

Well, these are the examples, two on each side: the Inquisitors and Kirk Sessions on the one hand; Hamilton and Bonhoeffer on the other. But now we come to the difficulty — how do we distinguish between the authentic and the perverted? How can we tell when we or other people are acting as genuine watchmen for God, or as interfering oppressors? On the face of it and from our perspective, it's easy to see that the Inquisitors were wrong and Patrick Hamilton was right. But these are extreme cases. It's not so easy to establish a test which we can apply to our everyday lives. We could say that love is the test. But then the Inquisitors sincerely thought they were motivated by love — love for God and love for the souls of the heretics. We could say that if the watchman uses violence, then he puts himself in the wrong. But then what about Bonhoeffer? Is it always wrong to kill?

Faced with these difficulties, many people consciously or unconsciously repudiate the role of watchman, and they take refuge in an entirely private kind of Christianity. Their faith, their religion, is a matter, they say, between them and God. They will not interfere with anyone else, provided they are left in peace. But that kind of private Christianity, or laissez faire Christianity, is not Christianity at all. It has lost its heart, its kernel. It has ceased to care, and therefore it has ceased to love. As the first letter of John says, you can't love God unless you love one another.

So we can't just turn our backs on the problem. We are all, like Ezekiel, appointed watchmen, we all have a responsibility for each other, and therefore we have to try to interpret how we are to discharge that responsibility, how we are to distinguish between oppressively interfering and genuinely helping.

There is one practical test which is quite useful. It's often said mockingly that the Calvinistic attitude to morality is that if you enjoy something it must be wrong. Well, you can apply that quite successfully to your role as watchman. It's difficult, for example, to avoid the impression that the zealous members of the Kirk Sessions who rounded up fornicators and adulterers and sabbath-breakers got a distinct kick out of what they were doing. So, if in your concern for someone else you're acting against your own interests, you're more likely to be on the right track. But that's a rough and ready test, it's scarcely an infallible one.

A better approach in interpreting your role as Christian watchman is to be very suspicious of the exclusiveness of your access to God, and of the exhaustiveness of your understanding of God. Don't think too highly of yourself as a Christian. Be flexible and diffident in your relationships with other people.

For example, in 1554 a man called Castellio of Basel wrote a book *Concerning Heretics*, in which he argued that Christians do not know enough to justify persecuting others for having different opinions. And a century later Oliver Cromwell, that sternest and most convinced of Puritans, found it necessary to say to the General Assembly of the Church of Scotland, in the quaint language of the day: 'I beseech you in the bowels of Christ, think it possible you may be mistaken'. Well, I don't know whether it is possible for a General Assembly to be mistaken, but that is what we should always say to ourselves about our own understanding of things divine when it comes to inflicting it on other people: 'I beseech you in the bowels of Christ, think it possible you may be mistaken'.

In other words, what I'm saying is this: let your role as watchman be liberating, not oppressive; let it be tentative, not dogmatic; let it open up others to the possibilities of God, rather than confining them to narrow certainties. The history of Christian theology in the last century has, I think, been the history of a progressive reduction in the content of Christianity. It is becoming increasingly difficult to say what a Christian believes, in terms of an exhaustive and infallible creed. And that, while it is frightening, is all to the good. It is of course much easier to see faith as a series of propositions, to which you give unqualified assent, even if you're not sure what they mean. But faith is not like that. Faith cannot be encapsulated in any kind of creed or statement. Faith is a living relationship with the living God, in which nothing is final, or certain, or infallible, except the relationship itself.

And when we watch over other people what we're concerned to do is not to impose our understanding, not to substitute ourselves for God, but to help other people to enter into their own relationship with God, to help them to their own faith. Because, as Paul says, each one of us must work out our own salvation in fear and trembling.

$\mathcal{S}in$

$\mathcal{I}$ want to speak to you this morning about sin.

That can be a dangerous thing to do, if one makes a habit of it. I once saw a cartoon in a church magazine which showed two women talking at a street corner, and one was saying to the other: 'I never knew what sin was until the new minister came!' And to preach regularly on the subject of sin is the mark of a certain type of evangelical approach, which operates by first making the victims acutely conscious of their sinfulness, and then stepping in to save them.

Of course this is not entirely wrong, because it was after all what Jesus himself was doing, according to the New Testament's summary of his message: 'Repent, and believe the gospel'. But where the approach becomes dangerous and distorted is, I think, in its understanding of sin. Christians generally tend to be rather unimaginative on the subject. If you look at the records of the Kirk Sessions in Scotland for the hundred years after the Reformation, you find that almost every punishable offence involved either sabbath-breaking or sex. In fact there seems to have been an obsession with sex. And three centuries later, William James (the brother of the novelist Henry James) wrote a very influential book called *The Varieties of Religious Experience*, in which he quotes several contemporary accounts of religious conversion — and almost all of them refer to the resulting liberation from the shackles of drink or tobacco.

One of them, for example, is by the son of a clergyman, who had reacted to his religious upbringing in the way clergymen's sons usually do. Since leaving Oxford he had, as he puts it, never darkened the door of a church again; and he spent his life drinking and gambling and generally living it up, until on a hot July day at precisely three o'clock in the afternoon he was converted. He describes this experience in moving terms and then goes on: 'From that hour drink has had no terrors for me: I never touch it, never want it. The same thing occurred with my pipe: after being a regular smoker from my twelfth year the desire for it went at once, and has never returned. So with every other known sin, the deliverance in each case being permanent and complete'.

I wish I could have met this gentleman and asked him what his authority was for the proposition that pipe-smoking is a sin — because the implication of all this is that if you remove the temptations of sex, alcohol and nicotine everyone will be good in the sight of God. It should be enough simply to state this proposition for its absurdity to be obvious. But I'm pretty sure that if you stopped someone in the street and asked them what they meant by sin, the answer would contain a reference to one of the three, if not all. That is what I mean about lack of imagination when it comes to sin. I think there must be laughter in heaven over it.

The solution, however, is not simply to change the list or to increase it. I suppose if we sent round a questionnaire after the service this morning, asking people for examples of sin apart from sex, alcohol and tobacco, we would get quite a varied response. Some of the answers would be indistinguishable from crimes: things like theft, or murder, or perjury — which might lead one to suppose that to live a law-abiding life makes one good in the sight of God. But can that be right? Is the Christian life simply a matter of obeying the law of the land? A more thoughtful answer to the question would broaden things out a bit, to embrace the ethical dimension: so that coveting one's neighbour's possessions would be included in the list, or swearing, or telling lies. But then, where does one stop?

The Jews at the time of Jesus, it would be fair to say, didn't know where to stop. They had the entirely laudable aim of making their lives free from sin, but in order to achieve that aim they produced endless lists of rules and regulations which were designed to cover almost every conceivable aspect of their daily lives. Religion became a matter of obedience, and of course the conclusion was almost inevitably drawn that if you obeyed all the rules you would be perfect in the sight of God.

And this made the Jewish religion on the face of it very attractive. You knew exactly where you stood with God, in fact you had him in your pocket, so long as you obeyed the rules. And you knew exactly where you stood with other people: the sinner, the outcast, was the person who had broken the rules, and you could measure the extent of his sin very precisely. If he was a really bad sinner, you would be justified in having nothing to do with him: indeed it was one of the rules that you should have nothing to do with him.

But on to this comfortable scene erupted the figure of Jesus, telling people about a different sort of God altogether — an unexpected God, a God who turns things upside down, a God whose values are apparently quite different from conventional human values, a God who doesn't turn away from sinners in disgust, a God who loves.

Because love has nothing to do with law and obedience to law. Law operates by definition. And when you define something, you exclude something else: a law defines what is permissible, and excludes what is not permissible. So once you start trying to define our relationship with God in terms of laws and rules and regulations, you automatically and unavoidably exclude some part of human behaviour from that relationship.

But the God whom Jesus came to reveal to us cannot be excluded, because he is a God of love, and love doesn't operate by defining and excluding. Love is an absolute, all-embracing thing, and the love of God reaches every corner of our existence. We respond to it not by obedience — which inevitably involves keeping part of ourselves back — but by surrendering ourselves up to the love of God, by loving in return.

And this means that we can no longer rely on our achievements, we can no longer point to all the rules we have obeyed and congratulate ourselves on our saintliness; nor can we point to those who have obviously broken the rules and call them sinners. We are all sinners. Jesus came to tell us to repent of our sin, certainly: but by 'sin' he meant not disobedience to religious rules; he meant, I think, the kind of self-sufficiency which turns its back on the love of God. Sin is simply doing without God. And paradoxically it is often the most religious people who are the greatest sinners in this sense.

That is why Paul and later Luther were against the Law. They saw that reliance on Law, or obedience to Law, far from bringing you closer to God, actually gets in the way and makes it impossible for you to understand the love of God and surrender yourself up to it. If you understand religion in terms of obedience, then you cannot love God — you can only fear him.

It was the love of God that Jesus was intent on showing us: in his teaching, in his parables, in his mixing with prostitutes and sinners. And we have in turn to reflect that love to modern outsiders. That, in a nutshell, is what it means to be a Christian: to be aware of the love of God, to respond to it, and to reflect it.

But this is not, I'm afraid, how Christianity is perceived by those outside the churches. When I was a parish minister in Edinburgh, I had on one occasion to go to a service of induction of a new minister in a very rough part of the city — a housing estate with a very high rate of unemployment and deprivation. I didn't know where the church was, and I drove round and round the dilapidated streets — empty except for the occasional gang of urchins breaking windows. When I eventually found the church I was already late, and as I walked up the path to the door I could hear the sound of the first hymn inside — and nothing could have been more incongruous in these surroundings. I was wearing a dog-collar because it was a presbytery event and there would be a procession at the beginning of the service, with all the ministers wearing robes and gowns and so on; but of course I had missed that now. And just as I reached the door of the church an old man went past the gate. He was a wild old man, with streaming white hair and a flapping greatcoat, and he was staggering a little; and as he went past, and saw my dog-collar, he brandished his fist at me and shouted out one word. I won't offend you by repeating that word in church: enough to say that it is a fairly common word in Australia, and it was intended to cast doubt on my legitimacy, and indeed on that of all ministers, because he used the plural.

Slightly shaken, I went into the church and sat at the back. And in the course of the next hour, as I watched the solemn and self-satisfied faces of the Presbytery at the front, and listened to the archaic forms of speech in the prayers, and to a very long and repetitive sermon, I came to the conclusion that the old man was right: not just about ministers, but about the church generally. We are all suspect, our legitimacy as Christians is in doubt, we are denying our inheritance. We cannot be true children of God unless we remember that the church exists, not for its own benefit, but for the benefit of others, of outsiders, of sinners — sinners in the real sense of being without God. And unless we remember this, we are ourselves godless — without God — because we can only find God through other people: through loving them, and having compassion on them, and caring for them.

I saw a film a few years ago which tried to imagine the life of Christ as it would have been in modern Glasgow. The disciples were all labourers, some of them unemployed, some of them thugs. And Jesus came from the same sort of background. But he didn't try to convert them in the sense of making them all turn pious, and give up their drink and their cigarettes and their women, and start going to church. Instead he spent his time with them in the pubs of Glasgow, a glass in one hand and a cigarette in the other, and he talked to them. He pitied them because of the emptiness of their lives, because of their despair, and somehow he persuaded them to turn round and see another dimension, which some people call God.

It is that Jesus whom we follow: the man who identifies with us in the meaninglessness of our lives, who joins us in our despair and points to the way out, and who excludes no one — no one at all.

The Spirit

$\mathcal{I}$N the old days the village school in Scotland used to be visited regularly by the minister, and the children were tested on their religious knowledge. And on one such occasion the class was to recite the Apostles' Creed by heart, each boy or girl saying a sentence of it in turn. Things began very confidently: the first child got up and said, 'I believe in God the Father Almighty, maker of heaven and earth', and then the next got up and said, 'And in Jesus Christ his only son, our Lord', and so on, and everything went like clockwork until they came to the bit where the Creed says, 'I believe in the Holy Spirit'. And at that point there was dead silence, until a timid voice said, 'Please sir, the boy who believes in the Holy Spirit is absent'.

I wonder how many there are present in our churches today who believe in the Holy Spirit. Of course we hear a great deal about it: the Holy Spirit is referred to constantly in our services, in our hymns, in the readings from the Bible, in the benediction. But constant repetition of an idea does not necessarily make the idea any more intelligible. In a church where the minister was in the habit of asking the children questions every Sunday from the pulpit, one child developed the technique of always shouting out 'Jesus', whatever the question was. Experience had indicated that with this answer he had at least a fifty per cent chance of being correct. In rather the same way, when I was studying theology one of my fellow students was always bringing in the Holy Spirit. Whatever the circumstances, whatever the problem, the answer was always the Holy Spirit. In Luther's words, you got the impression that he had swallowed the Holy Spirit, feathers and all. In fact among the more irreverent students he was nicknamed the Holy Spirit. But when a concept is overworked like that it becomes so diluted, its field of reference becomes so wide, that it ends up with no content, no meaning at all.

This then seems to be the general predicament of the church: either the Spirit is conspicuous by its absence, or it monopolises everything.

Now obviously there is something wrong with the first extreme, and many people are acutely aware of the lack of a spiritual dimension to their church life; they're aware that without that dimension the church is reduced to a social or charitable institution. This awareness is at the root of all revivalist movements. Clearly you cannot have Christianity without some understanding of the Spirit.

But, you might say, it's not so clear what is wrong with the other extreme: why should the Holy Spirit not dominate our lives and control everything we are and do?

There is currently a series of articles in a theological magazine, entitled 'First Aid in Pastoral Care', and this month the area in need of first aid is the Charismatic Movement. In the experience of the writer, the Charismatic Movement produces a unique type of spiritual and emotional casualty, which demands a distinct form of pastoral care. Of course in many cases it may be difficult to determine whether the spiritual group has wrecked the person's life, or whether the person joined the spiritual group because of a life already wrecked. And it is certainly true that many of those who do join such groups are inadequate, and are trying to find something to compensate for the lack of direction or meaning in their lives.

But it is also true that people in that position are very vulnerable to manipulation and control, and it seems to be the case that the leaders of spiritual groups are often tempted to assume such authoritarian control. The result is that people joining a spiritual group in a search for identity can actually lose their entire personality. Any doubts, any expression of their individuality, are discouraged as being evidence of ego-resistance; so that they end up as mere puppets, speaking by rote the language of the group, possessed and controlled by it. What has happened is that such people, who may have left their church in order to search for the Spirit, as for something external, have indeed found something external, into which they have been swallowed up. But it is not the Spirit of God.

That it is not the Spirit of God can be apparent not only from the destruction of a member's personality, but also from the exclusive attitude such groups frequently adopt. I have heard people who refer to themselves as 'we Spirit-people', implying that everyone else is a second-class Christian at best, and that the Spirit is something to be paraded: it's a badge which sets them apart from ordinary mortals, almost like a new circumcision; it's the external authority by which they act and think and speak.

All this is a kind of perversion of the Spirit of God. The Spirit of God is not something which is located outside us. You don't have to leave your church and go looking for people who talk about nothing else. You don't have to surrender your personality and your individuality and your own vision of God to an external authority who will tell you what to believe and how to express it.

The quest for the Holy Spirit is, rather, an internal one, which each of you can and must pursue right where you are, and for yourselves. No one can do it for you. I read and hear of ministers whose saintliness and spirituality are a byword among their flocks, and I sometimes despair of my own lack of distinction in either of these directions. But then I remind myself that the minister's function is not to be more saintly and more spiritual than anyone else in the congregation, as if the congregation could get into heaven by hanging on to his gown; as if salvation were a team effort and having a good centre-forward could save you from relegation.

The minister's function is not a vicarious one, as if he were a substitute for Christ, or as if, like the High Priest in Israel, he were the only one allowed to enter the holy of holies. The minister's function is actually to make himself superfluous, to remove himself from between you and God. He is there simply to take down the barriers of misunderstanding or prejudice or fear or guilt which may exist between you and God, so that you may see God and be reconciled to him; so that you may be conscious of the Spirit of God in your hearts and respond to it. The minister does not dispense the Spirit of God: he is merely a flunkey who tries to open doors and help to reveal God.

There is a passage in the letter to the Ephesians where the writer prays that his readers might be given the spirit of wisdom and revelation so that they might know God, so that 'the eyes of their hearts might be enlightened'. That arresting metaphor, the eyes of the heart, captures the inward nature of the Spirit of God. It recalls the great prophecy of Jeremiah: 'Behold the days are coming, says the Lord, when I will make a new covenant with Israel: I will put my law within them, and I will write it upon their hearts, and I will be their God and they shall be my people. And no longer shall each man teach his neighbour and each his brother saying, "Know the Lord", for they shall all know me, from the least of them to the greatest'. This promise, says the New Testament, has been fulfilled in Jesus, in the gift through Jesus of the Spirit of God, to those with eyes to see; or as Jesus himself says, to those with ears to hear.

In fact, hearing is perhaps an even better analogy to how the Spirit operates. The word for Spirit in both Hebrew and Greek means wind as well. Jesus says to Nicodemus: 'The wind blows where it will, and you hear the sound of it, but you do not know whence it comes or whither it goes; so it is with everyone who is born of the Spirit'. You cannot see it, but you can hear the sound of it.

Those of you who play a musical instrument will know that it is possible to play a piece of music without hearing it at all. You go through the motions as a purely mechanical exercise, which can indeed be quite therapeutic because your mind is blank while you're doing it, but you're not making music. The remedy for this is simple enough. My first music teacher used to say it ten times every lesson: 'Listen to the music!' I didn't realise then that it was possible to play music without listening to it, because everything was new and fresh to me. And so I thought it was rather a stupid thing to keep repeating. But then as I advanced I learnt the truth of it. As I got better, I got worse: better at playing, worse at listening.

And even the very best musicians have always to be reminding themselves to listen. Conductors when they're rehearsing an orchestra will often show how they want something played by singing it. Some of the great conductors have had pretty uninspiring voices: Barbirolli, for example, when he sang, sounded almost as if he were tone deaf. But if he really wanted to get across how he thought the piece should be performed he would pick up the nearest cello — because the cello was his instrument — and play and sing at the same time. It sounded like a virtuoso accompanying a cow. But that illustrates how you have to play music. The commonest word on the lips of the great conductors is 'sing'. You must sing inwardly as you play: only then do you hear the music yourself, and allow others to hear it as it should be heard.

In the same way we can come to church and go through the motions in a purely mechanical, ritualistic way, and go home again without having heard anything of the Spirit of God. The Holy Spirit is God's music, and to be a Christian is to play God's music. To play it you have to hear it, and to hear it you have to sing it. Now you can be taught to sing, but no one can sing for you. And in the last resort you can't learn from anyone else what the Spirit of God is. The Spirit is where you are alone before God; it is where God meets you.

Christians

$\mathcal{T}$ODAY I want to ask the question 'What is a Christian?' It's hardly a new question. I suppose in a sense the first person to ask it was the lawyer who said to Jesus: 'Teacher, what shall I do to inherit eternal life?' And ever since then the church has been asking itself the question, 'What is a Christian?', and formulating creeds or statements of belief in answer. It is a perennial question.

But what kind of question is it? Let me place it alongside some of the questions I had to answer in the last national census [in Britain]. First, I was asked whether I was married and whether I had children. These questions were directed to my legal status. There was nothing ambiguous about them; the answers were objectively verifiable, by looking up marriage and birth certificates. And by answering them with a Yes, I was at once put in the same category as everyone else who answered with a Yes.

Second, I was asked what my nationality was. The answer was that I was a Scotsman: I was born in Scotland, my parents were Scottish, I lived in Scotland. So I was at once put in the same category as all other Scotsmen.

Third, I was asked what my profession was. Well, at that time I was a solicitor, and I had various paper qualifications to prove it: one piece of paper which said I had passed certain exams; another piece of paper which said I had sat in an office for two years, ostensibly learning the trade. I therefore immediately belonged to the same category as every other solicitor.

So in each of these three categories — married status, nationality, and profession — there was nothing to distinguish me from anyone else in the same categories. The first category, married men, included both drunkards who regularly beat their wives and assaulted their children, and model fathers who devoted themselves to their family's well-being. The second category, Scotsmen, included both those whose ancestors fought with Robert the Bruce, and those unfortunate boat-people who a year or two earlier had been citizens of Vietnam. The third category, solicitors, included both the person just out of his apprenticeship who scarcely knew his way to the courts, and the family solicitor of fifty years' standing.

In other words, in each case the census was concerned only with the legal minimum necessary to admit you to that category. It wasn't in the least interested in what kind of father I was, or how patriotic I was, or whether I actually knew any law. If I had had difficulty in understanding any of the questions — if I had asked What is a solicitor?, or What is a Scotsman?, or Am I legally married? — then the answer would have been easy to find. The legal minimum for each case is clearly set out somewhere: it's just a question of knowing where to look it up.

But there was another question in the census form, which asked what religion I was. Now what kind of question was that? Did it have the same sort of status as the other questions? If I put down Christian, what exactly did I mean? In what way could my claim be verified — where could I look up the word Christian and find out what minimum qualifications were necessary before I could be admitted to that category? Well, I didn't lose sleep over it: I didn't consider it likely that the census people would come round and cross-examine me on whether I was really a Christian. I just filled it in and that was that.

But I wonder how many people who gave the same answer really stopped to think. Most of them probably just answered the question in a commonsense sort of way, as if it were the same type of question as all the others, on the basis that if you could say, 'I was born in Scotland, therefore I'm a Scotsman', you could in the same way argue, 'I was brought up in the church, therefore I'm a Christian'. If you could say, 'I have a marriage certificate which proves I'm married', you could in the same way argue, 'I'm on the roll of the local church, which proves that I'm a Christian'. If you could say, 'I have a degree in law which entitles me to be called a lawyer', you could in the same way argue, 'I lead an upright moral life, which entitles me to be called a Christian'.

Now these were very much the sort of arguments which the Jews employed at the time of Jesus to bolster up their religious self-confidence, their sense of their own standing in the eyes of God. And they were the sort of arguments which Jesus spent most of his time trying to destroy. Jesus was concerned above all to undermine the Jews' misplaced self-confidence before God, their understanding of religion as a matter of external qualifications, their interpretation of morality as the fulfilment of certain minimum obligations.

In John's gospel Jesus tells the Jews that the truth will make them free, and they answer indignantly: 'We are descendants of Abraham, and have never been in bondage to anyone'. Our religion is our heritage, they imply, our national possession: we don't need you, God is already on our side. In effect they're saying to Jesus: 'You're preaching to the converted'; and of course the most difficult people to convert are those who think they're already converted.

And not only did the Jews tend to think that they possessed God as a matter of course, by virtue of having been born into the chosen people; they tended also to think that their duty to God was simply a matter of obeying rules and regulations. Over the centuries, they had developed and extended the various laws in the Old Testament until they covered almost every aspect of daily life. Almost. That was the point. No system of rules and regulations, however detailed and elaborate, could be exhaustive. There was always something happening, some situation, which had not been expressly provided for. And the Jewish mind tended to think that if something was not expressly forbidden, then it was permitted. In other words their religion, their relationship to God, was becoming externalised, a matter of credit and debit, which could in theory be recorded and looked up, like the law itself.

Jesus's attitude to all this is contained in the great antitheses in the Sermon on the Mount. 'You have heard it said of old, You shall not kill... But I say to you, everyone who is angry with his brother shall be liable to judgement'. 'You have heard it said of old, You shall not commit adultery... But I say to you that everyone who looks at a woman lustfully has already committed adultery with her in his heart'. Jesus makes everything internal, he drives everything back into our hearts. Christianity is not a religion of minimum qualifications. It's not a question of finding out what is forbidden and what is permitted. It's a question of being open to God, allowing God into your heart. God has an absolute claim on you; it's not a claim which can be encapsulated in books of rules and regulations, however many you compile.

Now it's easy to sneer at these first century Jews with their externalism and legalism. But we're the same: we all want cut and dried answers; we all think how nice it would be to have our marching orders, so that being a Christian would be simply a matter of doing what we were told. What we want more than anything is to be told what to believe and what to do, so that when we see the question in the census form, 'What religion are you?', we can answer it as categorically and straightforwardly as all the other questions. That's what the Jews were trying to do: they were trying to make their religion systematic; they were trying to cut God down to size, to reduce him to manageable proportions. And that's what the lawyer was trying to do when he asked Jesus: 'What must I do to inherit eternal life?'

Well, Jesus makes him answer his own question in the words of the great commandment: 'You shall love the Lord your God with all your heart, and with all your soul, and with all your strength, and with all your mind'. In other words, God demands everything you've got. Or rather, love demands everything you've got. You can't love God with only a part of yourself, you can't hold anything back, otherwise it's not love. To love God is to give him everything.

And it's the same with ethics, with the other great commandment: 'Love your neighbour as yourself'. When the lawyer says in exasperation, in typical lawyer fashion, trying to pin Jesus down, 'But who is my neighbour?', Jesus doesn't answer. Instead he tells the parable of the Good Samaritan. Anyone, everyone, is your neighbour; whoever you meet, whoever needs you is your neighbour. You can't draw up a list, you can't define the category of neighbour, you can't exclude anyone; just as, in your relationship with God, you can't draw up a list of his claims upon you, you can't exclude anything.

It's a hard thing, this being a Christian, this doing without external props. And we're constantly trying to supply external props, whether in the shape of more precise statements of belief or more detailed instructions on how the Christian should behave. And people outside the church are constantly asking us to be more explicit about what we believe, about what being a Christian involves. Christianity would probably be much more successful — measuring success in terms of numbers — if it agreed to adopt a very specific statement of belief and programme of action. People generally want to be told what to do and believe, and they think that our unwillingness to do so results from confusion and lack of faith.

But Christianity is indefinable, and perhaps even essentially incommunicable. To try to answer the question 'What is a Christian?' is, as Kierkegaard would say, to try to paint the god Mars in the armour which made him invisible. To the extent that we define Christianity we betray it. The most that can be said is that Christianity is openness to God and other people, and so far as we elaborate on that we diminish this openness.

And it follows from such a requirement of continuous openness to the living God and to one's ever-changing neighbour that no one is ever a Christian, in the sense of having arrived at a completed status, like a chrysalis having become a butterfly. There are no fully paid-up members of the church. Christians are always in the process of becoming Christians: they must always live in the tension between being Christians, and being not yet Christians. In a paradoxical way, Christians must renounce the possibility of ever being Christians. Their Christianity is always an approximation.

Bibliolatry

$\mathcal{M}$Y subject today is idolatry — the worship of idols. And that probably sounds rather daunting. Idolatry is not a term we're familiar with nowadays; we hear it only on the lips of protestant fanatics. But a few hundred years ago, if I'd said I was going to preach on idolatry you would all have settled back comfortably in your seats — in fact you would have been rather uncomfortable if I'd preached about anything else. For example, idolatry was probably John Knox's favourite word. All his enemies, and he had many, were guilty of it. Indeed it sometimes seems as if they were guilty of idolatry simply by virtue of being his enemies. But of course Knox's Bible was essentially the Old Testament, and in the Old Testament he could find all the ammunition he wanted and all the precedent he needed for whipping up his followers to violence against this deadly sin.

In Geneva in the year 1558 he wrote what he called an Appellation to the Nobility and Estates of Scotland, with the object of persuading true believers that it was their duty to punish with death anyone who taught false doctrine. Naturally he quoted this passage from Deuteronomy:

> If your brother, or your son, or your daughter, or the wife of your bosom, or your friend who is as your own soul, entices you secretly, saying, 'Let us go and serve other gods',

you shall not yield to him or listen to him, nor shall your eye pity him, nor shall you spare him, nor shall you conceal him; but you shall kill him; your hand shall be first against him to put him to death, and afterwards the hand of all the people. You shall stone him to death with stones, because he sought to draw you away from the Lord your God.

Any protestant therefore, Knox implies, obviously has the right to kill any catholic, and it is the collective duty of all protestants to exterminate the catholics en masse. The Appellation goes on at great length, and as one of Knox's less sympathetic biographers says, 'He succeeds by a miracle of ingenuity in being at once monstrous and boring'.

I'm afraid that this would be a fair description of many of the hell-fire sermons of our ancestors: they succeeded in being at once monstrous and boring, and it must have been by a miracle of ingenuity because everything was said in the name of Christ. Indeed Knox closes his barbaric and bloodthirsty appeal to the Scottish nobility with a prayer that the Holy Spirit might rule in their hearts and the spirit of Jesus Christ guide them to the end.

But our greater modern sensibility should not blind us to the fact that idolatry remains a sin. The Old Testament after all is part of the Christian Bible, and the Old Testament regards idolatry as probably the cardinal sin. We should certainly have the courage to reject the precepts of Deuteronomy on how to eradicate this sin, but we should nevertheless try to understand what is behind all this violence and why the problem of idolatry should be a kind of *leitmotif* throughout the Old Testament. Every Book has something to say about it; the whole history of Israel is a history of constant backsliding by God's rebellious people, constantly fashioning idols out of clay or wood or gold, constantly a-whoring after strange gods. It's not surprising that our ancestors found the Old Testament such a treasurehouse of invective. But we suffer from their legacy, because the very mention of the word idolatry makes us feel uncomfortable. It smacks of bigotry and puritanism, and of sermons at once monstrous and boring. And we prefer to change the subject and talk about love and compassion; because although it can often be boring to talk about love and compassion, it is rarely monstrous.

The subject of sin is in fact very unfashionable in Christian circles nowadays. And rightly so, if by sin we mean things like drinking and smoking, or even sexual activity — sexual activity, that is, considered in itself and unrelated to what it discloses about the persons involved. Sin is much deeper and much more dangerous than that sort of thing. And of course it is quite different from simply breaking the criminal law. Nevertheless many people seem to think that if they have no previous convictions either criminal or moral, then they are blameless. But as it says in the first letter of John: 'If we say that we have no sin, we deceive ourselves'. Because sin is in fact self-sufficiency, doing without God, misunderstanding God and therefore ourselves. And that is essentially what idolatry is: distorting the image of God, substituting an idol for him, or turning him into an idol and worshipping it instead.

And this explains both the constancy of the theme in the Old Testament and its continuing importance today. The word may be old-fashioned, but what it stands for is as prevalent now as it ever was. Yet in updating the concept, in applying it to the modern world, it is very easy to trivialise it and rob it of its sting. It's the convention in the pulpit nowadays to condemn materialism, and to see in cars and houses and washing machines and so on the equivalents to the household gods of ancient Israel. And I suppose that if you're so obsessed with buying a new bathroom suite that you have no time to think of anything else, then it is a kind of idolatry — but a very diluted and very harmless kind. Because idolatry becomes sinister, not when it substitutes for God some pathetic object from the material world, but when it slips in undetected and distorts the proper understanding of God — when it comes in the guise of religion and piety.

For example, John Knox's understanding and use of the Bible were probably much more idolatrous than the Roman Catholic mass he attacked so vitriolically, because in his hands the Bible ceased to be the living word of God and became instead something petrified in the far distant past, a fossilised justification for his anger and lust for blood. Whenever you lock God up in the past like this, and treat the Bible as a book of rules, to be applied indiscriminately in any age, you turn God into an idol. You begin to control him and manipulate him, and very soon, without your realising it, the idol you have put in his place begins to manipulate you.

In fact our attitudes to the Bible are probably the best evidence of the continuing vitality and irrationality of this sin of idolatry. One of the most absurd examples concerns the history of the Greek New Testament. The first printed edition of the Greek Testament was produced in Spain in 1514, but for some reason it wasn't circulated to the public until 1522. And in the interval, the great humanist Erasmus managed to get his own edition both printed and circulated. It was a rushed job, clearly intended to beat the Spanish edition to the post, and Erasmus himself described it as 'precipitated rather than edited'. It contained hundreds of errors, and someone else described it much later as the most faulty book ever produced. Most significantly, the Greek manuscripts of the New Testament which Erasmus used in precipitating this edition were both late and inferior — indeed for the Book of Revelation he had only one manuscript available, dating from the twelfth century, and from this manuscript the final page was missing. So when he got to that point he simply translated the accepted Latin text into Greek.

But throughout the rest of the sixteenth century practically every printed edition of the Greek New Testament was based on that haphazard edition of Erasmus. It represents the text used by the translators of our Authorised or King James Version, and it was regarded with ever-increasing respect until, by 1633, it could be described in the preface to a new edition as 'the text which is now received by all'. And thereafter, for the next two hundred years, it was referred to as the Textus Receptus, the received text.

During those two hundred years, of course, scholars made enormous strides in the discovery and collation of ancient Greek manuscripts of the New Testament, so that the flaws in Erasmus's edition became more and more apparent. But because of the extraordinary and totally misplaced reverence paid to the Received Text, no new printed edition was allowed to tamper with it. All the newly discovered manuscript evidence had to be relegated to footnotes. At least one theologian was hounded from his university post for threatening to publish a new and more scholarly text. And right up to the end of the nineteenth century people were prepared to fight, slander and condemn on the basis of an edition of the Greek text whose origins were entirely fortuitous and whose quality was patently inferior.

This is idolatry at its worst: in the name of religion putting on a pedestal something so obviously man-made and so obviously full of human errors, and using the authority of God both to bolster it up and to stifle the voice of truth.

Truth, like the ancient Israelites themselves, is nomadic; it's always on the move. But human nature is always trying to capture it, we're always trying to pitch camp and put down roots and domesticate the truth. Idolatry is not limited to the Old Testament, or to people like John Knox, or to academic questions like the Greek New Testament. You meet it all the time. Here in this church some elders resigned in the 1890s because an organ was to be installed; in the 1950s some elders resigned because the organ was to be taken out. People complain when they're confronted with a new edition of the hymn-book, or a new translation of the Bible.

On a more important level, look at the question of the ordination of women. I read an extraordinary article last week in one of the more reactionary English newspapers, entitled 'Spare us, O Lord, the female of the species'. It could have been written by John Knox. And its main argument against the ordination of women was that 'Anglicans go to church for old times' sake, out of reverence for the ancient ways, out of habit, and they would no more welcome a woman at the altar than they would a foreigner on the throne'.

Has the world gone mad? No, it has only remained idolatrous. Because whenever we try to keep God imprisoned in the past we commit the sin of idolatry, we are bowing the knee to a spurious authority and turning our backs on the living God. The living God is on the move, and we are always trying to shoot him down. We are religious taxidermists: we want God stuffed and mounted where we can admire him and show him off, and so that we can know just where he is.

The Old Testament sometimes talks about God as if he had wings. But we should not think of the wings of a butterfly, transfixed in a glass case. That is idolatry, however beautiful it may be. We should think rather of that passage after the Exodus, where God says to Moses: 'You have seen what I did to the Egyptians, how I bore you on eagles' wings and brought you to myself'. God is on the move, and we must move with him and towards him.

Faith

ONE of the things it's sometimes hard to accept about the Bible is that it doesn't consist entirely of eye-witness accounts written down on the spot. It's not like the newspapers we read, when we can be sure that the account of the latest bloodbath or famine has been composed there and then by 'our correspondent'. The stories in the gospels about the life and teaching of Jesus were first written down quite a long time after his death.

To begin with they circulated orally — people heard these stories and passed them on, and not only would they be embellished and exaggerated as all stories are in the telling, they would also take on the distinctive outlook of the narrator. In other words the churches, the local groups of Christians throughout Palestine and the Middle East, shaped and moulded the traditions they received; they understood the stories in a certain way, and therefore consciously and unconsciously they altered the emphasis in order to reinforce that understanding.

And one of the chief tasks of New Testament scholars is to try to work their way back from the end product — from these stories as they exist in our Bible today — back through the historical process of alteration and accretion and exaggeration, to the earliest layer in the tradition: back as close as possible to the historical Jesus. And this of course is immensely difficult, indeed it is a task which in the nature of the case can never be completed. You can never be sure that you have arrived back at what actually happened, what was actually said. The most you can hope for is to be able to identify the authentic flavour of Jesus's teaching, the atmosphere, the style, the essence of the message which Jesus was proclaiming about God.

But sometimes you come across a passage in the gospels which strikes an immediate chord: there is something almost indefinable about it which bears the mark of authenticity. You feel instinctively that this is how it must have happened. When you read it you seem to hear the voice of history, you seem to see the scene before your eyes; it seems to capture the essence of an encounter so vividly and so arrestingly that you can only accept it as genuine. And the description in Mark 9:14-29 of the healing of the deaf and dumb boy is one of these passages.

Mark wrote his gospel in Greek, but it's a down to earth, unliterary, spontaneous sort of Greek, full of rough, common words, and uncomplicated constructions, which suits the immediacy of the gospel stories. There's nothing polished or reflective about his Greek, just as there is nothing polished or reflective about the sort of encounters Jesus had with the ordinary men and women of Galilee.

And the flavour of Mark's Greek is perfectly captured in the translation into Scots by the late Professor Lorimer, who was professor of Greek in St Andrew's University. It resurrects the spontaneity, the freshness of the gospel stories, which had been overlaid and stifled by the beautiful, sonorous, literary language of our traditional translations. As Professor Lorimer said, Jesus didn't speak standard Aramaic, the equivalent of our Queen's English: he spoke 'plain, braid Galilee'; and the translation into Scots puts us in touch once again with the authentic voice of Jesus and his contemporaries.

And nowhere more so, I think, than in this story about the deaf and dumb boy. Jesus comes down from the mountain with Peter, James and John, to rejoin the other disciples. And he finds them in the midst of a muckle thrang (a great crowd). 'What's your threap about?' (what are you discussing with them), he asks them, and a man in the crowd comes forward and tells Jesus about his son who has a tung-tackit (dumb) spirit. He had brought his son to Jesus, he says, but he couldn't find him, so he asked the disciples to cast out the spirit, but they couldna. So Jesus tells the man to bring the child to him, and whenever the child sees Jesus it falls to the ground and rows about faemin at the mou (rolls about foaming at the mouth). Jesus says: 'Hou lang time hes he been this gate?' (how long has he had this). 'Frae he wis a littlan' (from childhood), says the father.

There's something about that question and answer in the Scots tongue that brings out all the pathos in the scene — the compassion on the part of Jesus and the desperation on the father's part. And the father in his despair goes on: 'But gin ye can dae ocht, tak pitie on us an help us!' (if you can do anything, take pity on us and help us). 'Can?', says Jesus. 'Hae faith, an ye can dae aathing'. (All things are possible to him who believes.)

And then the father utters the words which in a way express the essence of the encounter between man and God, words which have echoed down over the centuries and still strike a responsive chord in our hearts today: 'I hae faith: help ye my want o it!' (I believe; help my unbelief.) And then Jesus heals the boy. Finally, at the end of the scene, the disciples ask Jesus privately why they hadn't been able to cast out the evil spirit, to which Jesus replies: 'This kind canna be pitten out bi onie mean but prayer'. (This kind cannot be driven out by anything but prayer.)

Now what did Jesus mean by that? 'This kind of spirit can only be cast out by prayer'. Prayer on whose part? He can't have meant prayer by the disciples — that would imply that the disciples normally cast out spirits on their own authority, automatically, without having to pray, but when it came to particularly obdurate spirits then they had to turn to God and ask for his help. That can't be right. So it must be a question of prayer by the person asking for help — in this case the father of the boy, the callan's faither. So that what the father said — 'I hae faith, help ye my want o it!' — is in effect described by Jesus as the prayer which led to the casting out of the evil spirit. It signalled the opening up of the father's heart and mind to the power of Jesus.

This little sentence, this cry of mingled hope and despair, is really the epitome of prayer; it sums up our relationship to God. Everything else, all our other prayers, indeed all our thoughts about God, all our theology, can be seen simply as footnotes to this one sentence, at once response and plea: 'Lord, I believe, help thou my unbelief'.

Compare this prayer of the callan's faither with the prayers of the hypocrites whom Jesus castigates in the Sermon on the Mount, who love to stand in the synagogues and at the street corners so that men can see them. Compare this prayer of the callan's faither with the prayers of the Pharisees, who thought that by their much speaking they would be heard by God. Compare the callan's faither with Burns's Holy Willie, whose prayer combines exultation at his own salvation with petitions for the damnation of his enemies. Compare this prayer of the callan's faither with some of our own prayers, the repetition of old forms, the ill-considered requests for trivialities.

This prayer, 'Lord, I believe, help my unbelief' — there is nothing premeditated about it, nothing calculating. It is wrung out of the man by the situation he finds himself in. He finds himself lost, threatened, with no one else to turn to. He has tried everything — even the disciples. I suppose we could say that even the church has let him down. He's alone with his despair, and in this frantic state Jesus confronts him, and he is now alone before God — because the crowds seem to melt away at this point in the story, leaving Jesus and the man facing each other, both then in their historical particularity, and now, today, here, because the callan's faither is you and me too. This is how we all find ourselves sooner or later, alone before God, with no one else to turn to, having exhausted all other possibilities. And Jesus says to the man: 'Hou lang time hes he been this gate?' 'Frae he wis a littlan', says the father, 'but gin ye can dae ocht, tak pitie on us an help us!' He has come to God, he has brought his wretchedness and laid it at God's feet and said, do something, pity me, help me if you can.

If you can. It's still on the human level, this encounter. The father has come to God as a last resort, but he still sees God as the highest among human possibilities. He still doesn't realise who he's dealing with.

Now, says Jesus, what's this about 'can'? With God all things are possible: hae faith, an ye can dae aathing. This encounter, he's saying, is no longer on a human level. You're not simply asking for something to be done for you. You're entering into a new relationship in which everything appears in a new light. Have faith.

And this is where the man's response is not only from the depths, but very deep in its insight into his own situation. I have faith, he says, but it's not enough. I believe, but at the same time I disbelieve. Help my want of faith, help my unbelief. He knows he can't get there by himself, he can't pull himself up by his own bootlaces to God's level. All he can do is bring his despair before God — to that extent he has faith; but the faith that can move mountains, the faith that enables you to dae aathing — that faith is beyond him.

One of the perennial problems in the history of Christianity has been this question of our role in our own salvation. Can we come to God and have faith as a result of our own efforts? Or is even our faith implanted in us by God, is everything the result of grace? It's a problem that has exercised the minds of Christians since the early centuries. And in our own day the dispute continues. Some theologians think that there is enough in our natural world and circumstances to raise in our minds the question of God and to make us turn to him. The opposite camp denies that we can have any religious impulse that hasn't been sown in us by God, so that even the consciousness of our lack of God implies the presence of God.

Now there's something slightly absurd about the whole business of laying down rules in advance about how God can act. When I began to study theology I didn't know what to believe about God. That was why I wanted to study theology — to find out about him. But people used to say to me: 'It's no use, you know. You'll never find God like this, you're going about it the wrong way round. You're beginning with understanding and seeking faith, whereas as St Anselm knew, and everyone knows now, you must start off with faith and seek understanding'.

That used to depress me and bewilder me. It bewildered me because I wondered how people could know with so much certainty about God's methods; and it depressed me because it seemed to reduce the question of faith to a game with well-defined rules, and all you had to do to win the game was to stick to the rules. I could not believe that Christianity was simply a game, or a system.

And I still don't believe it. The prayer of the callan's faither shows us what happens in reality. It is faith in action, not in the theologian's study. It shows us that in every Christian, faith is both present and absent. None of us has complete faith. So it is absurd to think that we can first have faith, and get that out of the way so to speak, and then concentrate on understanding. The two can't be compartmentalised like that. Faith is always in the process of being perfected — it's not a possession, like an entrance certificate to heaven. The man of faith is always asking God to help his want o it — and indeed one of the ways in which faith is helped and filled out is precisely through understanding.

And it's just as absurd to waste our time trying to decide who acts first in the process of faith — whether everything comes from God or whether we can take the first steps. In the eyes of the common man, this is like the philosophers who wrestle with the problem of whether motion is possible. The common man simply gets up and walks, and the problem is solved.

So it is with faith. The callan's faither doesn't bother his head with whether his coming to Jesus was God's idea or his own. All he knows is that he has come, and that he has faith, but his faith is not enough. God has to supplement it, to strengthen it, to make up his want o it. In his case it's not faith seeking understanding, it's faith seeking faith.

And that's what we're all doing, really, all our lives. This vivid scene so graphically described by Mark, so faithfully translated by Professor Lorimer, is not just a historical snapshot of an encounter in a far-off land at a far-off time. It is a parable of our own encounter with God, and it tells us how to approach God: it shows us how to articulate our despair. 'I hae faith, help ye my want o it!' In response to that prayer, God will cast out the deaf and dumb spirit which possesses all of us, and which, since we were littlans, has prevented us from hearing God's voice, and prevented us from raising our own voice to God.

Expectations

$\mathcal{T}$HE prayer this morning began with the words: 'Father, we don't know what to expect'. I last used this prayer at a service of induction at another church, partly out of a spirit of mischief, because of course it described exactly the predicament both of the congregation and of the new minister. I was hoist with my own petard, however, because I had not expected to have to switch on the public address system in the pulpit, and the result was that no one heard what I was saying.

But I had intended that both congregation and minister should ask themselves just what they were expecting and, further, that they should ask themselves whether they would be prepared to revise their expectations in the light of what they got. A new ministry, after all, is a bit like a blind date: there are risks on both sides, and there will no doubt be disappointments on both sides.

And the clearer and more specific the expectations, the greater the disappointment is likely to be. A minister who comes to a new congregation expecting everyone to want to study Hebrew will have to learn to adjust. Members of the congregation who expect the new minister to be a carbon copy of the old will probably leave. And of course if they feel an instinctive antipathy to the new man, if they find that he is actually a barrier between themselves and God, they are quite right to leave — just as it would be right for the minister to leave if he found that he was on a completely different wave-length from the great majority of the congregation.

But it is always wise before you take drastic action like that to consider your position in the light of the parable about the children in the market-place, and to ask yourself whether your expectations are legitimate:

> To what shall I compare this generation? It is like children sitting in the market-place, and calling to their playmates: 'We piped to you and you did not dance; we wailed and you did not mourn'. For John the Baptist came neither eating nor drinking, and they say, 'He has a demon'; and the Son of Man came eating and drinking, and they say, 'Behold, a glutton and a drunkard, a friend of tax-collectors and sinners!' (Matthew 11:16-19.)

What I mean is that when our expectations are not fulfilled, we should be prepared to question not only the person who fails to fulfil them, but the expectations themselves. When I lived in Dundee I knew a very religious couple called Paul and Georgina. They were very pious, and very evangelical, but they did not belong to any church. I asked Paul why this was, and he said that they had been to every church in Dundee over the years and had never found what they were looking for: nothing seemed to measure up to their expectations. So they just kept moving, a different church every week. In other words, they were prepared to challenge and find fault with every form of worship and every attempt to articulate God, but they were not prepared to challenge their own image and expectation of God. Like the children in the market-place they were calling the tune, and nowhere could they find a minister to dance to it.

Nevertheless I think there is hope for Paul and Georgina, just so long as they don't find what they're looking for. They are controlled by their expectations, and if they succeed in finding a minister who fulfils these expectations they will never escape from their stranglehold. For people like Paul and Georgina, a minister they disagree with profoundly is probably the best possible thing.

But I had a wider purpose in including in that induction service the prayer beginning 'Father, we don't know what to expect', because we are controlled by our expectations not only in respect of a new minister but also in respect of the church we belong to.

I have often heard people say that when they moved to a new area they tried several churches and eventually joined the one which was friendliest. Conversely, I have heard of several people who left a church because no one ever spoke to them, and then joined one where there was a welcome at the door and a smile in the pew. Indeed this kind of approach is so widespread that it has the status of conventional wisdom, and one hesitates to question it.

But the implication is that the expectations you come to church with are fulfillable by other people, not by God. God in fact doesn't really seem to come into it, except to the extent that he is understood to be present in a handshake and a smile of welcome. The music, the prayers, the preaching, any sense of the presence of God in the service — all seem to be irrelevant. If they do exist, they are simply bonuses. The important thing is the friendly atmosphere.

Now of course I don't say that friendliness is unimportant, or that we should not smile and welcome each other. I simply say that it is sad if these are the expectations people bring with them to church. And I think it illustrates the danger of having one's expectations fulfilled. We find our friendly church — and we go no further in our search for God.

After all, why do we come to church? Do we come to meet each other, and to have our understanding of Christian behaviour confirmed? Or do we come to meet the unknown God, to be confronted by him and challenged by him, and to acknowledge the inadequacy and fallibility of our presuppositions about him? Do we come to church because we know what to expect and because the church is somewhere we feel safe? Or do we come to worship the unexpected one, and to allow him to enter our lives in any way he may decide to?

And why do we come to communion? Do we come in order to keep up our record of attendance at church, or to pay lip-service to the centrality of the Lord's Supper in our tradition, or to join in the atmosphere of a church festival when there are more people than usual and it feels good? Or do we come because we do not understand the mystery of the sacrament, and we want to give God the chance to overcome our sluggishness and convince us through the bread and wine of his presence in our lives? Is our model the children in the market-place, who insisted on dictating the rules of the game? Or shall we imitate Jesus in the garden of Gethsemane, saying to God, 'Not what I want, but what you want'?

Because the real reason why I used this prayer at the induction service, and why I use it today, is that the controlling power of our expectations applies not only to our relationship with a new minister or with the church we belong to, but to our relationship with God.

We can say broadly that Jesus was put to death because the God he proclaimed did not conform to expectations. So that the parable of the children in the market-place is not just an isolated observation at a particular stage of his ministry: it enshrines a kind of *leitmotif* which applies throughout. People were always resisting Jesus because what he told them about God did not square with what their traditions and their habits of mind led them to expect.

The temptation scene in the wilderness at the beginning of the gospel strikes a kind of programmatic note; it is the overture setting out the themes which are going to dominate the whole work. Satan tells Jesus that all he needs to do is turn stones into bread, and summon angels to his aid, and conform to the sort of power structures which everyone operates with and understands. But Jesus rejects all that, and his ministry is a protracted contradiction of what everyone expects and wants. He spends his time with sinners, with the outcasts and misfits, with whores and collaborators. He not only breaks the rules of the Jewish religion: he undermines all rules by implying that any formulation is inadequate, and that only an internal and absolute obedience can do justice to God. He performs miracles, but then refuses to make capital out of them, by insisting that they should not be publicised. And then of course he goes and dies the death of a criminal. The sort of death the more reactionary among us would like to see terrorists and child murderers condemned to is the sort of death which comes to the son of God.

It's hardly surprising that his fellow Jews, confronted with this contradiction of all their expectations, should have responded in the way they did. All their upbringing, all their inherited traditions, must have seemed to conflict with the God whom Jesus revealed. And we are always tempted to destroy what we do not expect and do not understand.

Because if all this was true of the Jews, it is true of us too. If the Jews were the product of tradition, so are we, and tradition is a dangerous thing. The long history of our faith, stretching back to the days of the New Testament, is a mixed blessing. In many ways it supports and nourishes us, and points us in the direction of God. But in other ways it constricts us and imprisons us, because it forces us into a preconceived and outdated mould. It insists that we understand God in terms of structures and images and metaphors which may once have been entirely legitimate, but are no longer so. The danger of tradition is that we will be so controlled by our history that we will be led to try to control God in turn, and insist that he fulfil our expectations.

And when I talk about the stranglehold of tradition I mean not just ways of talking about God and worshipping him which have grown up in our church here over the past hundred and fifty years, and not just the religion and theology we have inherited from the wider Church of Scotland, or even from the whole church universal since the days of Constantine the Great. It applies right at the root of things, to the creeds and confessions, and to the New Testament itself. Only if we can bring ourselves to see the New Testament as a collection of human responses to God in Christ, on the same level in principle as our own potential response, only then will we be free to make our own response, uncontrolled by the expectations and presuppositions which are forced on us by tradition.

Luther and the Reformers wanted to escape from the stranglehold of the traditions of the church by going back to the New Testament. Their slogan was *sola scriptura* — scripture alone. But that wasn't radical enough. We have to escape from the stranglehold of scripture, and force our way through to the living Christ. Perhaps that sounds blasphemous, but it is in accord with the belief that the Bible is the word of God. Because if that is true, that the Bible is the word of God, then it means that the Bible is not exhaustive. The word of God is 'living and active, sharper than any two-edged sword': it is not to be confined to the pages of a book, however holy, however inspired and inspiring.

The Bible is a record of how people responded to God over the course of a thousand years or more, and particularly a record of how people responded to what happened in Jesus. It is not the end of that response, nor should it control all future responses to God and to Christ, in the sense of limiting either God's freedom to approach us or our freedom to respond.

Each of us is called to make our own response to God. Each of us has to be our own evangelist, required both to respond and to proclaim. But we can only genuinely respond to God and adequately proclaim him if we make room for him and allow him to be who he is, and not just what we expect him to be. And we have to make room for Jesus, to allow him to be who he is: not the triumphant ascended saviour of the world, whom centuries of tradition encourage us to imagine sitting at the right hand of God in a geographical heaven we can no longer believe in; but the suffering son of man who came right into our human condition and shared our predicament to the point of being abandoned by this totally unexpected God. Because that Jesus still comes to us, in the most unexpected ways: in pain, in despair, in other people — and not just the people we love.

We will never see God if we think we know what he looks like. We will never hear God if we think we know his voice. Only if we allow him his freedom to do anything with us, and to come to us in any way he chooses, will we ever be able to respond to him. We don't know what to expect — and that is God's greatest gift to us.

Beginnings

$\mathscr{I}$T used to be said that Scotland was really a pagan country, because the Scots attached more importance to New Year than to Christmas. Things have changed a bit, and Christmas is now generally celebrated with equal enthusiasm, but it is certainly true that New Year's Day was originally a pagan festival. All the ancient peoples observed it — Egyptians, Persians, Babylonians, Jews, Greeks, Romans. It seemed to satisfy some deep-seated need in human beings for renewal. It corresponded to the cycle of nature, to spring and rebirth and hope. For the Romans it was a time for exchanging presents, which were intended as omens of good luck for the coming year. Our own ancestors, in case the luck didn't materialise, took the additional precaution of bribing the magistrates on New Year's Day. But for everyone it meant a chance to turn their backs on the past and on all their failures and shame and disappointment, and make a new beginning.

Now what significance should we give to such a festival within Christianity? At first sight it seems to be simply a hangover from the pagan past — like some of the amulets which have survived from Germanic tribes in the Dark Ages who had been forcibly converted to Christianity. Some of these amulets are decorated with figures of local gods, others have the crucifix, others have a combination. For the first generation after conversion the local gods were probably still venerated, under a veneer of Christianity; later on they would have receded into the background, but would still linger in the memory — there would still be a superstitious fear of parting company with them entirely.

I imagine it's the same to some extent with our New Year. It has nothing really to do with the Christian calendar, but it still speaks to that deep psychological need for renewal, so the churches feel that they should respect it and have special services in its honour. And that's not a bad thing. It's always a mistake to drive a wedge between Christianity and deep-seated human needs. But it is a greater mistake to allow deep-seated human needs to control and shape Christianity. We have to recognise the correspondence between the human psychology and the cycle of nature, but at the same time we have to resist reducing Christianity to the status of one of the mystery religions which were so prevalent at the time of Jesus, and which promised rebirth and resurrection on the basis of nature myths, like the annual return of Osiris or Persephone from the kingdom of the dead.

Christianity does promise new beginnings, but there is nothing mythical or cyclical about its foundation. Its foundation is historical: it is the life and death of a particular man at a specific point in history. Of course, in the life of any Christian believer there is a beginning in another sense, a subjective beginning, a renewal or rebirth of some kind in his personal existence; but no real Christian experience can so to speak take off, unless it has its point of departure in the historical events recorded in the New Testament.

But there the problems start. The temptation is always to look at the Bible in the same way as a lawyer looks at a statute. There may have been case-law subsequently which will give him some idea how the statute has been interpreted, but ultimately he will always go back to the precise wording of the statute — that will be the controlling factor. And we've been encouraged in this kind of attitude to the Bible by the Reformers. One of the principal areas of conflict between Luther and the papacy was the question of authority. The Roman church of course attached great weight to the Bible, but only as it had been interpreted down the centuries by the church. Ultimately, authority lay in that tradition. Over against this, Luther set up the principle of *sola scriptura* — scripture alone. The only controlling factor is whether or not you can find authority in the Bible.

And this was quite a useful criterion, so long as it was simply a question of ridding the church of some of its more obvious and absurd distortions. But when it was a question of deciding positively what to believe and how to act, it was not so successful. Scripture as ultimate authority could very easily become as inhibiting an influence as ecclesiastical tradition. If you read Calvin's Institutes, you find yourself constantly irritated by the way he breaks off an argument just when it's getting interesting, by quoting some text of scripture and treating it as sufficient proof of his proposition simply because it's there in the Bible. It's irritating because our understanding of God will never advance if, for example, what the Psalmist said three thousand years ago — perhaps in a totally different context — is regarded as the final word on the matter. In this way the Bible can actually become a barrier instead of an aid to revelation.

And of course even Luther did not entirely believe in his slogan, scripture alone. His historical sense was too acute, and in practice he made distinctions between the books of the New Testament, describing for example the letter of James as 'an epistle of straw' which should have no weight beside the letters of Paul. Now when you begin to talk like that, you're admitting a new and overriding criterion. It's no longer scripture alone that counts, it's what you think of scripture. You've opened the door to criticism — logical, historical, and theological criticism.

And in the field of criticism we've come a very long way since the Reformation. It has become possible, and I think advisable, to look at the New Testament no longer as a divinely dictated book which has the last word on any subject to do with man's relationship to God, but as a collection of very human responses to the man Jesus. It records the beginnings of Christianity, but not the end: it is not the last word on the matter, and it should not control us to the extent of muzzling us and preventing us from making our own responses, in our own perhaps very different and indeed even contradictory terms.

There are, after all, very different and even contradictory

responses within the New Testament itself. The four gospels for example give quite separate accounts of the life and person of Jesus. In the old days people used to produce so-called harmonies of the gospels, in which all the differences were ironed out and the discrepancies removed. But what these harmonies failed to recognise were the totally different atmospheres which the various gospel writers convey.

The Jesus of John's gospel, who makes long and profound speeches about his relationship with the Father, is quite different from the Jesus of Mark's gospel, who rarely utters more than two or three terse sentences at a time. The description which Mark gives of the disciples is quite different from that of Luke: in Mark they are obstinate, obtuse, and unreliable, whereas Luke has nothing derogatory to say about them.

But all this does not mean that one version is true and the other untrue. We now recognize that the writers of the gospels were not trying to write factual biographies or histories in our modern sense. In fact such things did not exist then, even in the secular world. Modern historians try to present the facts objectively and then add their interpretations. Ancient historians short-circuited the process: they put across their interpretation in the way they presented the facts. So that Mark, when he describes the dull-wittedness of the disciples, is trying to tell us something about the message of Jesus and the response it elicits — he's not telling us something about the disciples which the other gospel writers did not know.

In this way each gospel is conditioned by the theological reflection of its author, and those authors are all human beings, of the same status as ourselves, so that we are at liberty both to make our own equivalent response, and if necessary to reject any particular aspect of their response in favour of a different one — just as Luther felt impelled to reject the response embodied in the epistle of James.

But then of course behind all this theological reflection there is the question what these writers were responding to: in other words, the question of the historical Jesus. Surely, you will say, the gospels contain some eye-witness accounts, some authentic memories of what Jesus said and did. Well, this is what many scholars have tried to recover. They have tried to identify those parts of the gospels which can be attributed to the period since

Jesus — whether accumulations or exaggerations in the hand-ing-on process, or the theological reflections of the gospel writ-ers — and having identified these, they subtract them, and what they are left with is allegedly Jesus as he really was.

The trouble is that even the material which has been handed down to the gospel writers is itself in the nature of a response: it has received its peculiar character by a process of selection, or partial omission, or alteration of emphasis or context. There is in fact no such thing as a purely objective eye-witness account.

This is common knowledge to those who spend their lives in the law-courts. The one thing you never arrive at in the courts is the 'truth'. You may succeed in eliminating deliberate falsehood, but you can never be satisfied that you have estab-lished what really happened. What you do is produce a hypothesis, and if you can persuade the court that the evidence approximates to that hypothesis, then you may have proved your case. But the oath which witnesses take in court, to tell the truth, the whole truth, and nothing but the truth — that is a pious fiction.

I'll give you a trivial example. When I broke my ankle last month, I did so on the front doorstep at midday in front of my wife and our neighbour. The next day we were discussing what had happened, and I said that I had fallen on the right-hand side of the concrete path; the neighbour said I had fallen on the left-hand side; and my wife said it wasn't on the concrete at all, it was on the gravel at the side of the path. Now of course I was right and they were wrong, but that's not the point. Each of us was convinced, and certainly there was no question of any deliberate falsehood. We had each responded in a different way to a specific event, and none of us could describe to the satis-faction of the others the way it had really happened. There is no doubt that something happened, but whatever it was it was only accessible through the filter of human experience.

It is surely the same with the beginnings of Christianity. We cannot get at the historical Jesus as something prior to and sepa-rate from the evidence about him in the New Testament. Everything we know about him is in terms of the response of other people. We have to keep going back to the New Testament in case our faith degenerates into wishful thinking, a figment of our imagination corresponding to a universal human need. But we have also to keep reminding ourselves that the biblical evidence is human evidence. The Bible is not a book of magic spells, which makes any further mental effort superfluous; nor is it a sort of child's pop-up book, from which Jesus springs up as he was when he walked the earth; nor is it a statute-book, which precludes us from making free inquiry and arriving at our own responses. The Bible is necessary, but it is not sufficient.

Because we do have another kind of access to Jesus. Christianity began in the New Testament, but it also begins in the life of each Christian, and it takes its beginnings in this sense from the presence of the living Christ, just as it did in the lives of those who wrote the books of the New Testament. I say the presence of the living Christ: you could talk about the spirit of God in Christ; or if you find language like this difficult and unhelpful you could use words like intuition, or insight, or religious imagination.

The important thing is that you should recognise both the limitations of the human insights recorded in the Bible, and the potential of your own insight. We tend in the protestant tradition to inflate the Bible and deflate ourselves, and then we do justice to neither. If you want to begin to be a Christian — and all of us are always starting out afresh — you must do justice to both kinds of beginning: the historical beginnings in the New Testament, and the personal beginnings in yourself. Each will provide a check on the other, but only if you acknowledge both the humanity in the Bible and the divinity in yourself.

Rules

$\mathcal{W}$HEN I came here last year I spoke about rules, and about how important I thought it was to break them. Of course it wasn't quite as simple as that: if it had been I probably wouldn't have been asked back this year. But this year I'm going to take the risk again, because I intend to speak about the same thing: the importance of breaking rules. You might think that this argues some kind of obsession on my part with rules, and you might be right, but there are two reasons why I'm beginning to make a habit of talking to you about them.

The first reason is that you live together in a school, an institution, and all institutional life is determined by its attitude to rules. There may be fewer rules nowadays than there were when I was at school, and the punishments for breaking them may be less startling, but your lives are still controlled to a very great extent by rules. So it's important that you should have as healthy an approach to them as possible. And the second reason is that Christianity, being a religion of freedom, is also determined by its attitude to rules: negatively, that is, because what Jesus really came to tell us was that our relationship with God is not a matter of obeying rules and regulations.

In other words, a school, like any institution, depends upon rules for its existence, while Christianity tries to do away with rules. Putting the two together in that way might lead you to conclude that Christianity is impossible at school. I don't think things are quite as bad as that, but I do think that Christianity is by no means to be taken for granted in any institution. You have to work at it, and constantly question its true character, because whenever Christianity becomes identified with the institution, or with keeping the rules, then it loses its freedom and ceases to be Christianity.

A church, of course, is just as much an institution as a school, which means that with something like school chapel you have twice the problem. You have always to be asking yourself whether your understanding of Christianity comes in conflict with either the school rules or the chapel rules, or both.

The first time I became acutely aware of the problem was when I was in my last year at school. We used to have chapel on Sunday evenings and I used to sit at the end of the back row of the choir, squeezed into a corner beside the organ. One Sunday evening the minister was more than usually dreary. He had been droning on for about twenty minutes and showing no signs of letting up, and I was getting more and more bored and uncomfortable in my corner, when I suddenly found in my pocket a whistle, which I'd been using that afternoon to referee a rugby match. And whenever my fingers closed on it a terrible temptation formed itself in my mind, to put the whistle to my lips and blow it as loud and as long as I could, cutting into all the dull solemnity of the sermon and all the pious pomp and circumstance of the Sunday evening service. I would blow it, and then clamber over the organ and across the front of the chapel, and out and away for ever. Because of course I would be expelled. But what a way to go, what a protest, what a gesture!

For the next ten minutes I sat there in a cold sweat, my fingers locked round the whistle in my pocket, always just on the brink of raising it to my lips. I'm afraid you're going to be disappointed, indeed I've always been disappointed at myself, because I resisted the temptation. The sermon eventually ground to a halt, and we all filed out, and no one ever knew about my little interior drama until just now.

Now I realise of course that by telling you about it I'm asking for trouble: if any of you should happen to have a referee's whistle in your pocket it would be an ideal chance to put a stop to me droning on. I can't guarantee it, but I shouldn't think anything terribly serious would happen to you — you would only be practising what is being preached. The reason I mention it is that it sums up fairly well the tension I was talking about between the individual and the institution, between freedom and rules.

Of course if I had blown the whistle it wouldn't have been a particularly noble thing to do: I wouldn't have been sticking up for any principle, or drawing attention to anything worthwhile — I would simply have been drawing attention to myself. But the story is intended as a kind of parable: there will be times in your life when you will be very tempted to blow the whistle and put a stop to everything, even if it means disaster for yourself. And what you have to learn — what is really the art of life — is how to distinguish between when it's right to blow the whistle, and when it's wrong.

It's not easy: you won't find any rules about it, and you won't find anyone who can teach you. In fact you probably won't even find anyone to agree with you when you do finally summon up the courage to blow the whistle. After all, a referee's whistle is supposed to be blown when the rules of the game have been broken. The referee is supposed to uphold the rules and represent the establishment, the institution.

But the kind of whistle-blowing I'm recommending to you is itself a breach of the rules, and people who break the rules are not popular. They're a threat to the ordered life of the institution, and if they break enough rules the institution will eventually react by expelling them. So it is a serious and dangerous thing to do, and it's as well to be aware just how serious and how dangerous. But there will be times when you will find yourself in a corner with the whistle in your pocket, and you will have to decide what you're going to do.

Now when I said that you won't find anyone who can teach you how to decide, what I meant was a teacher in the ordinary sense of the word — a master in class, or a minister in the pulpit. But there is something that can help, and that is a kind of inner voice. The first reading this morning (Amos 7:10-17) described how the prophet Amos started to criticise the king of Israel. And the king's priest, a man called Amaziah, told Amos to go away and prophesy somewhere else, otherwise he would find himself in trouble. To which Amos answers simply: 'God said to me, Go, prophesy to my people Israel'. In other words, God said to Amos: 'Blow your whistle, and put a stop to all this nonsense in Israel'; while Amaziah said to Amos: 'Don't you dare blow your whistle. If you do, you're for it'.

The problem sounds simple enough: obviously you should listen to God rather than to Amaziah. The trouble is, how do you know which is God speaking? After all, Amaziah was a priest, apparently a man of God himself. He says to Amos: 'Don't prophesy here, in Bethel; this is a sanctuary, a temple of the Kingdom' — this is a church, you can't blow your whistle in here. Amos had to be very sure of himself, or rather he had to be very sure of God. He had to be sure that God was actually turning against the established religion — that God was breaking the rules.

That of course is a difficult thing to grasp and to accept — that *God* breaks the rules. But the second reading this morning, the parable of the workers in the vineyard (Matthew 20:1-16), is saying just that. The ones who started first thing in the morning and worked all day and in the heat of the day, queue up in the evening expecting to have their efforts rewarded. But they find they get exactly the same wage as the layabouts who only started at tea-time and only worked for a couple of hours. What kind of justice is that? It's all very well saying that the master only contracted to pay a certain wage and is sticking to it. The fact is that he's being unfair, it's not the sort of behaviour you would expect.

And that's the point. God, says Jesus, is not what you expect; he doesn't do what you want him to do, what you think he ought to do. God's standards are not your standards. You don't own him, you don't possess him, you can't dictate to him how he should behave. Your rules, however respected they are, however important they are for the smooth working of your institutions and your daily lives, are not the end of the story. God is not bound by your rules: he breaks them. Just when you're all sitting half asleep in the midst of your comfortable institutional life, he blows the whistle. But of course like all institutions you feel threatened, and you pretend it's not God at all who's blowing the whistle, but a rebel and an impostor, and you have him crucified.

Young
and Old

$\mathcal{D}$URING this last week I've been going every day to the General Assembly of the Church of Scotland. The Assembly meets once a year, when about 1300 ministers and elders from every part of Scotland come together in a big hall to discuss various things. This is the first time I've been a member, so that I was able to look at everything with fresh eyes.

And I'm sorry to say that there was only one thing about the Assembly that appealed to me. There is a little bell, and once anyone has been speaking for ten minutes somebody rings this bell and the speaker has to shut up. This is an excellent idea. My only criticism would be that ten minutes is an awfully long time. It's just about the length of one of my sermons, so you might say that this past week I've been getting a taste of my own medicine.

It's been immensely boring, and immensely uncomfortable because the seats are very hard. And you have to keep standing up when important people come in, dressed in peculiar costumes, and you have to bow to them. And people use very old-fashioned language, and there are rules about who can say what at any particular time, and no one really understands the rules except a handful of men who've been going to the Assembly for years and years, and they're the ones who do most of the talking: not because they're particularly good at it, or because they have anything very important to say, but because they just seem to like to hear the sound of their own voices, and if anyone else wants to speak it usually turns out to be against the rules.

So you can see that with the exception of the ten-minute bell, my reactions to the General Assembly have been rather negative.

Now it occurred to me as I was sitting there that what I felt about the Assembly must be very like what many young people feel about church. In your eyes the church seems to belong to the establishment, it seems to be under the control of a handful of people who've been in it for donkey's years, and apart from them no one really understands what's going on but nobody's allowed to change anything. The atmosphere belongs to another age, everything is solemn, some people wear funny clothes and look pompous and self-important. You have to sit on hard seats and listen to someone who doesn't know when to stop — and there isn't even a bell that rings after ten minutes. It's so boring that you get a tight feeling in your stomach and you want to scream.

If you feel like that, then you're normal, and to a large extent you're right. Very often it's only the young who look at things with fresh eyes, who see the truth.

But the answer is not just to walk away. I have to confess that on the first two days of the Assembly I did leave very early. The atmosphere was too oppressive — there was so much self-satisfaction. I came away each day saying to myself: 'Who do they think they are?'. I didn't really want to have anything to do with them. But then half-way through the week I realised that I was showing another, and this time less attractive, side of the young — I was closing my mind to what I disagreed with. I was acting on the principle: if you can't beat them, leave them. And that doesn't work — it simply leaves things in their hands so that they can do what they like.

I could just abandon the Assembly and let it continue on its old dreary course. But it is the voice of the church, it takes votes on things and makes decisions. Most of these decisions are unimportant, but a few are very important. If I wasn't even there to vote against what I disagreed with, then I would have no right to criticise it later. I was a member, and therefore responsible for what was decided. So I realised that I must sit it out, and hope that in the future, in the long term, I and people who think like me would be able to change things for the better.

It's the same principle with you and the church. Of course you can turn your backs and say: 'Forget it, it's boring and irrelevant and meaningless. We'll leave it to the old codgers'. But if God is important then the church is important, because the church is supposed to reflect God. If you abandon the church, then in some sense you abandon God. And you must not do that. You must come into the church, and if you disagree with it you must turn it upside down, and breathe fresh life into it so that it does reflect God. You must keep in touch with us, and keep talking to us, even if everything you say is rude.

Truth and Experience

*W*HEN you're young you have to take a great many things on trust. You have to assume that your teachers know what they're talking about, and that what they teach you is true. If you didn't assume that, you would never get off the ground. To begin with, of course, when you're very young, you don't even know that you're making such an assumption: you just accept everything unquestioningly. But later on, when you get a bit older, you begin to realise that not everything people tell you is true, because your experience says otherwise. And then you start accepting things provisionally. You say to yourself: 'Well, that's what the teacher says, and he's usually right, so I'll take it on trust for now; but when I can I'll test it against my own experience, and only then will I really know whether it's true or not'.

In some subjects it's relatively easy to apply the test of experience. If someone tells you that two plus two equals five it shouldn't take you long, with the aid of a few apples or fingers, to prove them wrong. It's the same with science. I probably know less about science than anyone else here, but I do know this: that everything in science has to be backed up by experiment.

We had a science master at school whose name was Fred, and none of his experiments ever worked. Whenever an explosion was expected it never came, and often when no explosion was expected he produced one. But he always ended up saying: 'Never mind, you'll just have to take my word for it'. And of course that's just what we should not have done. We should have insisted that he did every experiment over and over again until he got it right, otherwise we would refuse to believe him. Naturally we did not insist, and in any case old Fred had a terrible temper and told us we were stupid if we asked awkward questions.

Teachers, in my experience, are often like that: when they can't answer the question they tell you that you're stupid. Benjamin Franklin, who discovered electricity and had one of the most inventive minds ever, was regarded by his school teachers as abysmally stupid, because he kept asking questions like Why is lightning? Unfortunately there is no guarantee that if your teachers regard you as stupid then you're going to be a genius in later life; but it does mean that you should never be afraid to ask questions, you should never take things for granted.

With other subjects it's more difficult. You may have to wait longer before you can test what you've been told against your own experience. With French, for example, you may have to go and actually live in France before you realise that you were taught idioms which went out of fashion before the first world war. But the principle is the same: the most important thing you can learn is never to accept anything blindly and unquestioningly.

And this applies not just at school, and not just in relation to teachers. Of course in the outside world generally, you have to adopt this basic attitude of trust towards other people — otherwise you would never get anywhere. But it must be a provisional trust, subject to revision in the light of experience. And not only because some people you come across are going to be mistaken or even deliberately deceitful: it may be that the truth is something which they cannot tell you, because in some way it is bound up with you and you alone.

The philosopher Wittgenstein told a story about a traveller who stopped a passer-by and asked if he was on the right road for London. He was told that he was, but he never reached London, because the passer-by had omitted to tell him that he was facing in the wrong direction. The information was objectively true, but objective truth is not always enough: you must test everything against your own experience and your own predicament before you accept it as true for you.

Now what about religion? Well as a matter of fact this applies to religion more than to anything else. Partly because your own experience of God may be non-existent, and you may have to wait a very long time before you can put what other people say to the test; and partly because it is especially the case in religion that what other people claim to be true may be true for them but not true for you. The more certain a man is that he's had a religious experience, the more important that will be for him, and the more passionately he will insist on its validity. The trouble is that he will often insist on its validity for other people as well, and that doesn't necessarily follow.

There are, for example, many descriptions of religious experience in which people claim that they've been converted suddenly — at ten past nine in the morning on the second of June, or whatever. They suddenly saw the light, and life was never the same again. And this may well be true. But the implication of such claims can be that unless the same sort of thing has happened to you, then you know nothing of God and have no right even to call yourself a Christian. And that is nonsense. If anyone ever tells you what God is like, or who he is, or what you must expect of him, don't believe it — I mean don't accept it unquestioningly. If you respect the person, you may take it on trust for the time being; but always be prepared to throw it out, in the light of your own future experience of God — otherwise you may be shutting out God forever.

When I was in my first year at boarding school I was quite interested in God. I had no idea who he was but, judging from the services in chapel, God seemed to have something to do with the chancel. The chancel was a bit at the front end of the chapel, up a flight of steps; there were seats in it round the side, and a large gold cross on the wall. At the beginning of every service the masters trooped in, wearing their gowns and academic hoods, and solemnly climbed the steps into the chancel and took their seats. And at the end of the service the chaplain carried the collection up the steps into the chancel on a large gold plate and raised it above his head and then put it down in front of the gold cross. Mere boys were not allowed to go into the chancel, and the impression I got was that this was because they might contaminate it. It was clearly the holy of holies, and God was somehow more at home there than anywhere else.

One night I woke up at about three o'clock, and dared myself to get up and go down to the chapel. I don't know what put the idea into my head, and I found the prospect terrifying, but I forced myself to do it. I got out of bed, put on my slippers and dressing gown, went out of the sleeping dormitory, and made my way in pitch darkness along endless corridors and down stone spiral staircases, and into the chapel. There was a dim light coming through the stained-glass windows, and I made myself go through the chapel, and climb the steps into the chancel, and touch the gold cross. And then I found my way back to bed.

I don't think I realised then why I had done this — it just seemed a crazy sort of dare. But I know now that it was my instinctive way of proving to myself that there was nothing especially holy or sacrosanct about the chancel, that God did not live there, and that he was not inseparably bound up with the authority of the masters or with the mystique surrounding the dedication of the offering. The god who lived in the chancel was in fact an idol, and I had succeeded in unmasking it. I had satisfied myself that if I were to find the true God, I must look elsewhere.

But where? That I still can't answer. I know very little positively about God. I have had no vision of God: nothing, that is, like Isaiah's vision in the Temple. And that makes being a minister rather difficult. Because most people want to be told what to do and what to believe: they don't want to rely on their own experience. And they find that life is much easier if they do believe in idols, because they can control idols, they can keep them in their place, they know what to expect from them.

All I can do as a minister is try to cut some of the idols down to size, and to open people up to the possibility of experiencing God themselves; to clear the path between people and God, by getting rid of all the debris of misunderstanding which litters that path. There are so many misunderstandings: for example that God is someone who lays down rules and then punishes you for breaking them; or that sin is anything you like doing, and anything you like doing is sin; or that the Bible is a kind of statute-book, there to be obeyed. But the biggest misunderstanding of all is that God only comes to you in visions and blinding lights.

There is no limit to the ways God comes to us: he can come at any time, in any place, in any disguise; in success or in failure, in happiness or in disaster; suddenly, or so gradually that you don't even realise it. The only thing that will stop him coming, is when you pretend to yourself that you know all about him, or when you accept unquestioningly what other people tell you to expect.

At the beginning of this century there was a famous professor of philosophy in the University of Oxford, who used to address his first year students in these words: 'Gentlemen,' he would say (because in those days there were no female philosophers), 'you are now about to embark on a course of studies which will occupy you for three years. Together they form a noble adventure. But I would like to remind you of an important point. When you go down from the University, you will go into the church, or to the bar, or into parliament, or the army, or into industry or commerce, or into various other professions. But nothing you will learn in the course of your studies here will be of the slightest possible use to you in later life, save only in this: that if you work hard and intelligently, you should be able to detect when a man is talking rubbish — and that is the main purpose of education'.

I would add that it is perhaps even more important that you should be able to detect when you yourself are talking rubbish, or when you are thinking rubbish, or when your life is full of rubbish: in any of these events, God cannot get through to you. God operates most happily, I think, in silence and in space: you have to be silent so that you can hear him, and you have to make room for him.

I shall finish with two cautionary tales. The first on silence. The great conductor, Sir Henry Wood, described how he was once conducting a symphony by Beethoven, in which there is a sudden and intensely dramatic pause: after the full orchestra has been crashing away for several pages, suddenly there is complete silence for two whole bars. And on this occasion, when they reached the pause, Sir Henry heard a voice behind him in the front row of the audience saying: 'I always fry mine in dripping'. The point is that God comes to us in silence, in the still small voice — but if we are so engrossed in the trivia of our own lives, we won't even notice the silence.

The second cautionary tale is on space, on making room. It concerns another professor, a very learned professor, who went to consult a guru about Zen Buddhism. The guru offered him tea, and when the professor held out his cup the guru poured the tea and went on pouring long after the cup was overflowing. When the embarrassed professor eventually said, 'Look here, the cup's full', the guru said, 'So are you. You're full to overflowing with your own ideas, your own preconceptions, your own self. I can do nothing, until you have learnt to empty yourself'.

I hope that in your lives ahead you will give God the chance to be God: allow him the silence which he needs to be able to speak to you, and make room for him in your hearts and minds so that he can enter.

Suffering

$\mathcal{I}$ have used the parable of the rich fool more than once in my sermons, probably because it's one of the few parables I think I fully understand. I can identify with it, I can recognise the rich fool in myself — as I think we all can. It's not a question of money: it's a question of complacency and moral inertia, it's a question of being human and turning your back on God, it's a question of sin. Because sin is not so much wrong-doing as wrong thinking, having your mind set on the wrong things. The Greek word for sin means, literally, missing the mark; and that's what the rich fool does — his aim is wrong.

But there are other, less obvious ways of missing the mark, and one is to act what I would call the poor fool. The rich fool says to himself: 'I have nothing to worry about, I'll sit back and enjoy myself'. The poor fool says to himself: 'There is one big snag in my life: if only I could get rid of it, then I could sit back and enjoy myself'.

For example, I'm the sort of person who has an unerring gift for buying faulty things. Nothing I buy ever seems to work. I buy a foolproof fountain-pen, and it leaks; I buy a pair of shoes, and the next day they don't fit; I buy an umbrella, and the first rainy day it falls apart. And with mechanical things it's even worse. I seem to have the kiss of death — typewriters, lawn-mowers, and worst of all cars. Now if you're like that, you tend to be always saying to yourself, 'If only the typewriter hadn't broken down this morning, I'd be in a good mood'; or 'If only I could get rid of my car and buy a proper one, life would be worth living'. That, on a very mundane level, is how the poor fool's mind works: he is always thinking that if only things were different, then he'd be happy.

And of course it applies on deeper levels: on the level of sickness, and broken relationships, and death. 'If only I could be free of this pain', says the poor fool to himself; 'if only I hadn't quarrelled with my family; if only my wife were still alive'. In fact, what the poor fool really wants is to be a rich fool: he wants to be rid of his problems so that he can sit back and enjoy himself.

And I think that most people oscillate between the two positions: when things go well they are rich fools; when there is a blot on the horizon they are poor fools. What this implies is that most people are very confused about the problem of suffering — and by suffering I mean all the negative aspects of life: not just physical pain and death, but emotional problems, thwarted ambitions, financial worries, feelings of failure, and so on.

And people who are Christians — that is, followers of a religion which is based on the cross, the emblem of suffering — seem to be in general no less confused. There are, broadly speaking, three approaches among Christians. There is the rich fool, who may indeed sympathise with the afflicted, but is profoundly glad that he is not of their number; there is the poor fool, who is intent only on minimising his own suffering; and there is the ascetic, who has a morbid appetite for suffering, and sees it as his passport to heaven.

It is the first two that concern me most, because they imply a kind of living from hand to mouth spiritually, an inability to cope in advance with the problem of suffering: there seems to be no adequate theological framework to fit it into.

Having said that, I must add that there is a sense in which it is necessary and right to live spiritually from hand to mouth. Christianity is not a system, although it is often presented as if it were. Christianity is not a collection of cut-and-dried answers to the problem of suffering; and the Bible is not a kind of textbook of Christian ethics, which tells you what to do in any given situation, or how to cope when something ghastly happens to you. That kind of understanding of Christianity can cause a great deal of confusion and distress. People think they know the orthodox solutions to the problem of suffering, but when the crunch comes they are dismayed to find that the orthodox solutions don't work; and then they feel guilty or betrayed — they feel that their 'faith' has let them down, as if faith were a kind of magic charm which should carry them unscathed through all misfortunes.

Christianity is not a system, and the cross is not a principle: it's not a kind of new rule introduced in the year 30 AD into the game of life, which from then on you can't win unless you abide by it. That's how the ascetics see it: if you haven't already got a cross to bear, they say, go out and look for one — you won't get into heaven otherwise. In this way, God is perverted into a kind of insane tyrant. Instead of the Old Testament God, who created the world and saw that it was good and wanted his creatures to enjoy the world and each other — instead of that life-affirming God, you get the god of the ascetics, who rejoices only in pain, and rewards his creatures in proportion to their denial of his creation. That kind of approach doesn't attempt to make sense of the cross: it simply asserts the cross as a principle.

But I repeat: the cross is not a principle, and Christianity is not a system. You may have read recently about a Roman Catholic professor of moral theology in America, who has been silenced by the Vatican because he refuses to subscribe to the official teaching of the church. His argument is that in moral theology — Christian ethics — you can't have textbook solutions. You can't just look up the chapter on contraception or whatever and say, this is what everyone must do or not do. You must in every case have regard to the person involved: so that abortion is not always wrong, homosexuality is not necessarily a depraved aberration, premarital sex is not automatically unchristian, and so on. You can never state categorically in advance what is right and what is wrong.

So that really it becomes doubtful whether there is any such thing as Christian ethics, considered as a system. People often ask me for 'the Christian answer' in their predicament — for example, when they are trying to decide whether to get divorced, or whether to live together. The answer must be that there is no Christian answer — beyond perhaps Augustine's famous or infamous maxim: Love God, and do what you like.

In that case, you may be asking yourself, why have the church, why have ministers, if all they do is sit there saying 'There is no Christian answer'? And I suppose that's what worries the Vatican — people need answers to their problems, they need to be directed, they need to be told what is right and wrong.

But it seems to me that the function of the church is not to provide solutions or instructions, but to put people in touch with God, and that means, mainly, removing the barriers which already exist between people and God. Because although Christianity is not a system, according to which you can solve all your problems in advance, you can nevertheless say certain things in advance about God in relation to suffering, which can help to avoid misunderstanding and unnecessary pain and confusion.

You can say first of all that the traditional image of the transcendent God sitting up in heaven and keeping a kind of scorecard for each of his creatures, and wondering how he will next put their obedience to the test — you can say that this is an image which hardly does justice to the idea of a loving God, and which is hardly conducive to a healthy attitude to pain and suffering. If you think of God like that, then when disaster strikes you either reject him, treating such a deity — rightly in my view — as a tyrannical monster, or else you endure everything meekly for the sake of passing the test and getting the reward.

You may of course try to convince yourself that things are not as bad as they seem, by telling yourself that when one door closes another opens. That is a very common saying, and one which it is difficult to quarrel with because there does seem to be evidence to support it. But I don't think I agree with the usual implication, that it is God's doing.

When people repeat this saying — 'When one door closes another opens' — they are usually trying to let God off the hook; they are saying that he's not really such a tyrant, because he generally brings compensation of a sort in the wake of catastrophe. And that is sub-Christian. Carried to its logical conclusion it applies to the resurrection itself, which is then seen as simply compensation for the cross. It remains quite unclear why there had to be a cross in the first place.

It is true that very often one door opens when another closes — but not because of a kind of concession on the part of God. The real reason is the doggedness of the human spirit, which refuses to be put down, and is always battling to find some new way of expressing itself.

Now, I have objected to the concept of a purely transcendent God looking down at us from above, and I have asserted the importance and the essential nobility of the human spirit in the midst of suffering. But my conclusion from these premises is not some kind of humanism: my conclusion is that the true God is somehow down here with us, and that this is only really apparent when we suffer.

If that is the case, then it becomes possible to understand and even welcome suffering: not as involving some idiotic test, like the king in the fairytale sending out his daughter's suitors to perform impossible tasks before they can claim her hand; but as uniting us to God, as God and humanity joined together in the struggle against evil and in the perfecting of his creation. The cross then takes on quite a different aspect. If God was in Christ, then the cross represents this union of God and ourselves, joined in pain. It both embodies it historically, and symbolises it universally and forever.

And then the invitation to take up your cross and follow Jesus begins to make some sense. It doesn't mean, go round looking for crosses, or inventing them. It means, don't waste suffering: don't turn away from the challenge like the rich fool, and don't simply try to wish it away like the poor fool. Accept it, take it up, shoulder it: not with resignation as one of the rules of the game, as the entrance fee to a future paradise; but calmly, because it means that God is with you now, in the present, supporting you, fighting alongside you.

Incarnation

$\mathcal{T}$HE book of Ecclesiastes in the Old Testament has a certain beauty, but it is a melancholy, poignant sort of beauty. It seems to sum up the despair which began to afflict the philosophers of the Jewish religion in the period between the Exile and the birth of Christ. These so-called teachers of wisdom had an enormous thirst for knowledge and a natural instinct for things divine, yet they kept coming up against the bitter experiences of life, and all they could ultimately do was to articulate the contradiction: that man yearns for God and can never reach him. 'God has put eternity into man's mind, yet so that he cannot find out what God has done from beginning to end'. (3:11)

It expresses that deep sadness which seems to be characteristic of late antiquity. It's the sadness you see gazing out of the sightless eyes of ancient Greek sculptures: those perfectly formed monuments to human beauty and human art and the human spirit, which nevertheless exude not gaiety and life but a great hopelessness. All is vanity, says the preacher, all is vanity.

Now it is widely held that Christianity supersedes this saying in Ecclesiastes: 'God has put eternity into man's mind, yet so that he cannot find out what God has done from beginning to end'. You don't hear many sermons on Ecclesiastes, and when you do they tend to use it as an Aunt Sally. And many people hold to the position that the Bible is the word of God which tells us precisely what he has done from beginning to end.

I don't think the Bible is quite like that. I don't think that it represents a kind of hot-line to God, or that it contains all the answers. In fact I don't think that Christianity does supersede this saying in Ecclesiastes about the tension between man's thirst for eternity and the inscrutable mystery of God. I think it still holds, but with a slightly different slant.

I shall give you three illustrations from the world of music. Those of you who saw the film *Amadeus* will have been encouraged to believe that musical inspiration can be quite independent of personality. Mozart is portrayed as a boisterous adolescent with a manic giggle and a lavatorial sense of humour: and this unprepossessing youth produces a constant stream of sublime music. It's almost as if music is a divine liquid which God pours indiscriminately into the nearest available receptacle — and nectar presumably tastes the same whether it is in a gold cup or in a distinctly earthen vessel.

It's an old paradox, this. I remember when I was a music student there was a particularly obnoxious youth in the orchestra, who was conceited and bumptious and generally unpleasant, but at the same time he was one of the most outstanding horn-players I've ever heard. I could never quite understand how someone with such a repellent personality could play with such sensitivity and natural artistry that he regularly brought tears to people's eyes. And I deduced then, what most people must deduce from *Amadeus*, that there is simply no necessary connection between music and human personality.

But that is naive, just as the film was naive. Mozart's music is not superhuman, or extra-human, in the sense of being outside human experience. It seems divine only because of its effortlessness. In reality it encompasses the range of human emotions more completely and in a more down-to-earth and realistic way than almost any other music. It is sublime because of its humanity.

I remember that in a music appreciation class at school the master played the opening bars of Mozart's G minor symphony and asked us whether we thought it was happy or sad. I was so entranced by the music that I immediately said 'happy', and I was rather put out when I was given to understand that it was supposed to be sad. But in reality words like happy and sad are quite inappropriate to Mozart's music. The moods are so subtle and so fleeting, and the colours change so quickly, that you cannot pin them down with pedestrian labels and generalisations — and in this his music is true to life: it is profoundly human, and it is the product of his personality and his experience and his earth-bound vision of God.

On the island of Patmos there is a cave which tradition says was the residence of St John the Divine, the author of the Book of Revelation. Except that according to tradition 'author' is the wrong word, since the guide will show you the shelf in the rock which served as a seat for the angel who dictated every word to St John; and you can also see the mark on the stone floor where St John knelt as he wrote it all down. Whether that was indeed the case with St John, it was certainly not the case with Mozart. His music is not divine, it was not dictated by angels. It is, as the writer of a doctoral thesis is required to state in the preface, 'entirely his own work', and it bears the marks of his personality as clearly as the floor of the cave in Patmos bears the alleged imprint of the saint's knees.

Is there in fact any such thing as 'divine music'? Aldous Huxley thought there was: he considered Beethoven's A minor string quartet to be the sound of paradise. But Beethoven was further away than anyone from being a divine composer. His sketchbooks are the evidence of the most tortured methods of composition. On his deathbed he is said to have raised himself on his elbow and shaken his fist at heaven. He was a man, struggling to give expression to his need for eternity, but never denying his humanity in the process. He was Prometheus, trying to wrest secrets from the gods.

And thirdly, Mahler shows most clearly of all this alchemy at work, this transmutation of the base metal of human experience into gold. Mahler had a desperately unhappy childhood: his father was a drunkard and was always quarrelling with his wife and beating her. And one day, when Mahler was still a little boy, and his parents were engaged in a more than usually violent fight, he could stand it no longer and rushed out of the house; and in the street outside there was an organ-grinder who was churning out some commonplace tune over and over again. And in his symphonies Mahler is constantly taking a trivial folksong like 'Frere Jacques' and transforming it into a vast and profound structure, as if all his life he was haunted by the contradiction between the yearning for eternity and the brick wall of human experience. That is why his music is so bittersweet and expresses so well the sense of uprootedness and alienation which is characteristic of our century.

Now in each of these examples — in Mahler's banal material, in Beethoven's ferociously rewritten sketchbooks, and in Mozart's unbroken stream of masterpieces — the music is the result of the interaction of the divine and the human. And to each example you could apply the aphorism of Ecclesiastes: 'God has put eternity into man's mind, yet so that he cannot find out what God has done from beginning to end'.

But in the case of music I find this aphorism no longer melancholy and poignant, but a simple description of the human condition and of the foundation on which all music rests. There is no divine music; at least such a thing is inconceivable for us: how could there be music without conflict, without passion and yearning, without humanity? It is impossible to imagine a sort of ethereal, disembodied music of the spheres, just as it is impossible to imagine God without man.

And this is where Christianity has made the difference. In the light of Jesus, the aphorism in Ecclesiastes loses its poignancy: it is no longer a curse but a blessing. It simply describes the condition for the Christian life, and the limitations of humanity are now, as it were, sanctified. Christianity is not, like the ancient mystery religions, the revelation to the initiated of the divine secrets. Christianity is the journey towards God on which, paradoxically, God accompanies us. God is no longer the remote transcendent being he seemed to the author of Ecclesiastes. God has entered the lists, he came to us — he comes to us — in the man Jesus, which means that our lives like our music are a fusion of the divine and the human.

You cannot have God without man, any more than you can have divinely inspired music, or a Bible dictated by angels. That is not the way God works — if it were, there would have been no need for Jesus and the cross. God is accessible only through the human, so that we must learn both to accept our humanity and constantly to put against it the question mark of eternity. We will never solve this tension, any more than we will ever hear divine music. But we should be as thankful for the tension of the Christian life as we are for the sublime humanity of the music we do have.

$\mathcal{P}ossessing$ $\mathcal{G}od$

$\mathcal{T}$HERE is an attitude to God which is very widespread in church circles generally and which sees him as a possession, someone whom you can control and manipulate; you own him as of right, you've inherited him or entered into a contract with him, and you know just where he is and where you stand with him; if you scratch his back he'll scratch yours; you have him in your pocket.

I first came across this attitude in any pronounced form when I was studying theology at university. The students who had been brought up in what one might call conventional Christianity found themselves exposed for the first time to the critical onslaught of modern scholarship. They were presented for the first time with the necessity of being honest in their relationship with God, of going through with the questions which naturally occurred to them, and of accepting the answers which they were driven to. And they found themselves face to face with a different God, and a different Jesus, from the God and Jesus they had grown up with.

It must have been a very painful process, and some of them instinctively recoiled. They refused to allow their own private

God to be contaminated by this new approach; they retired into a sort of protective cocoon. During their three or four years at university, they went through the motions of going to lectures and sitting exams and churning out the answers that were expected of them, but in reality they were keeping their private God intact. They were only waiting for the time when they had got their degrees and qualified as ministers, when they could find a church of their own, and preach the religion which they had been born into, and which hadn't changed for them since they were at Sunday School.

I sympathised with these students, but I also found them extremely irritating. There seemed to be something smug about their attitude, smug and possessive and arrogant: they claimed to have a hot-line to God, a kind of private access which wasn't available to others. They knew God, it appeared, in an unshakeable and impregnable way. It wasn't the inspiring kind of faith which insists on God's goodness in the teeth of all adversity: it was more the kind of pigheadedness one associates with the Flat Earth Society. It wasn't so much an unquestioning faith, as an unquestionable faith — you weren't allowed to question it.

Now in contrast to this attitude, the university and the New Testament were beginning to reveal to me a different God: different not only from the kind of God I heard about in church but from every kind of God I could imagine, different in principle from all my expectations. The God whom Jesus showed us is in fact the unexpected God, who turns all our ideas on their heads, who explodes all our preconceptions and presuppositions. To claim to know him or possess him is like closing your fist on air. The only possible approach is one of openness — openness to his infinite possibilities, and to the possibility that we are wrong in everything we think we know about him.

This does not mean that Christianity is a kind of game, where the rule is that you must practise openness. Christianity is often reduced to the status of a game: in fact any system which is based on commandment and obedience very soon becomes a kind of game, and the most dignified reaction to that brand of Christianity is the atheist who simply says, 'I'm not playing'.

Take the so-called sin against the Holy Spirit, which can never be forgiven. There have been many candidates for this sin of sins in the last two thousand years, ranging from the sinister to the pathetic, from the profoundly evil to the absurdly neurotic. And many people have considered themselves literally beyond redemption as a result. But I'm sure that this is a ridiculous misunderstanding, ridiculous because it is so far from what Jesus intended.

Jesus had no one act in mind, however evil, however corrupt. What he did have in mind was the attitude which turns its back on the true nature of God. If you cannot bring yourself to accept the forgiveness of God, why then you will not be forgiven. It's not a question of rules in a game, it's a question of logic, indeed it's a tautology: you do not will to be forgiven, therefore you will not be forgiven. The sin against the Holy Spirit is the approach which denies the spirit of God, which misunderstands the nature of God.

So whenever you insist on preserving intact the God you are familiar with, at all costs, refusing to question him or to question yourself, refusing to open yourself to what you do not yet know of him — then you are committing the sin against the Holy Spirit. This doesn't mean of course that you're a lost soul and have no future. It simply means that so long as you don't change, so long as you remain shut up in your own prejudices — prejudgements — about God, then you are excluding the true God and preventing him from having any effect on you. Your possessiveness is an illusion: you possess nothing, because God cannot be possessed.

Of course, what happens when you think you possess God is that your God has become an idol, so that this widespread attitude I'm talking about is simply idolatry. Idolatry sounds a very old-fashioned thing: it's what John Knox used to find lurking under every bush, and it's what you see on sectarian posters during papal visits to Scotland, and therefore one hesitates to use the word in case one is dubbed a fanatical extremist. But I take the risk.

The word appears very often in the Old Testament; you might say it's the Old Testament sin of sins. The Israelites are always incurring the wrath of God for a-whoring after strange gods and worshipping idols made of wood or ivory or gold. It all seems pretty remote from our experience. But what lies behind it is a concern to preserve the freedom of God from all our attempts to imprison him within narrow limits.

And these attempts to imprison God are perennial: it's part of our make-up as human beings to want to control him, to turn our backs on the unpredictable, unexpected God who leads us into the wilderness, and to fashion an idol out of our familiar possessions and fall down and worship it instead. Only then do we feel comfortable and safe and secure. But there is nothing comfortable or safe or secure about the true God, or about Christianity. Indeed it almost comes to this, that it's when you're feeling at your most comfortable and safe and secure that the idol is most in the ascendant.

So when I refer to the conservative students I knew when I was at university, I'm only using them as an obvious example of this kind of idolatrous approach to God. Because in fact it's something we all share, even the most sophisticated of theologians, even the humblest of saints.

There's a man Harry Williams, who is now an Anglican monk and at one time was Dean of Trinity College, Cambridge, and who more than anyone else I know of qualifies both as a sophisticated theologian and as a humble saint. And in his autobiography he describes his own gradual liberation from that part of his God which was in reality an idol. His mother had been a keen evangelical, someone who referred to herself as 'out and out for Jesus': her method of evangelism was to whip up guilt feelings and then offer religion as a cure. So Harry Williams grew up to identify religion with guilt. God was someone who demanded attention and obedience, and if he didn't get it he was angry. Religion was in fact simply a neurotic compulsion.

Harry Williams served this idol for many years — long after he was ordained and a professional theologian. Then he had a dream in which he was at the theatre and something made him turn round: at the back of the theatre he saw a horrible monster which was hypnotising the actors on the stage. And he began to realise that in the same sort of way he himself was a slave to an idol-God, who was stunting his growth, and stifling his sexuality, and preying on his feelings of guilt and fear. But it took a catastrophic nervous breakdown and thirteen years of psycho-

117

analysis before he began to feel more or less free of the monster's clutches.

Sometimes in church I'm reminded of Harry Williams's dream, and I imagine an invisible idol standing behind me, hypnotising the congregation. Perhaps it's only imagination, but I suspect there's an element of truth in it. What I try to do as a minister is to enable you to escape from that hypnotic trance. I try to make the first crack in the pedestal, so that you can bring the idol crashing down, and open yourselves up to the true God in all his freshness and unexpectedness. It's not an easy thing to do, and it's not a popular thing to do: the idol naturally resents it, and so do the idol's worshippers — and each of us to some degree worships the idol. But although it's neither easy nor popular, there's nothing else worth doing from the pulpit. Everything else is simply grist to the idol's mill.

Families

A month ago I went to a baptism in Germany — in fact I was there as the godfather — and the form of the ceremony was much the same as ours has always been, except that the minister asked the parents and the godparents to come forward and stand round the font as he baptised the baby, so that they were visibly a family unity, within the wider family of the congregation. This seemed to emphasise rather well the significance of baptism as both sanctifying the human family and incorporating the child into Christianity.

Because the Christian church is by intention much more than just a community. Communities are of our making, whereas the family exists by the grace of God. For example, there's a church in Freudenstadt in the Black Forest which has an enormous fifteenth century crucifix on the front wall beside the pulpit, and the guidebook makes a great thing about the figure of the Christ on the cross, how its outstretched arms seem to welcome everyone who comes into the church, and to gather them up into the family of God.

But it's easy to get sentimental about the family, and baptismal symbols and formulae can easily become facile and superficial. Because there is another and darker side to the family. This same church in Freudenstadt is of very unusual design: it has two naves which stand at right angles to each other and join at the altar. Each nave has its own entrance, and no one sitting in one nave can see anyone sitting in the other. Only the minister in the pulpit can see into both naves. And the church was designed like this in order to separate the men from the women: there is a male nave and there is a female nave.

That is the other side to the family: although it is intended to stand for unity and love and self-denial, it has a kind of built-in tendency in the opposite direction. The family is a God-given thing: he intends by means of it to bring us together and embrace us. But instead it seems to breed divisions and disunity and pain.

Because there is more pain caused by distorted family relationships than by anything else. It's much the most widespread form of misery I see as a minister. Not bereavement or sickness — these bring more often than not a kind of dignity in sorrow, a kind of unlooked-for peace; if you like, a growth in moral stature. But the pain which results from broken families is a purely destructive thing, and it is terribly common.

Perhaps I'm overexposed to it, like the doctor who begins to wonder whether there are any healthy people left. But I think that the family which has no problems is very unusual. Everywhere there seem to be parents who feel neglected or insulted; sons and daughters who feel possessed or threatened; brothers or sisters who look back to some real or imagined grievance and nurse their wrath to keep it warm; and husbands and wives who feel betrayed or misunderstood or simply disappointed.

And the strange thing is that they all seem to think they're in the right. I hear so many allegations of outrageous behaviour, and it's very easy to accept them on their face value and apportion blame accordingly. Very easy and very dangerous.

In Scots law there are two obscure kinds of ownership rights called stillicide and emphyteusis. And Robert Louis Stevenson, who studied law much against his will, used to say in later life that the only two things he ever learnt about the law were that stillicide was not a crime and emphyteusis was not a disease. I sometimes think that the only thing I ever learnt from the law, not from the study of it but from the practice of it, was the truth of Augustine's maxim: *audi partem alteram* — hear the other side.

Always hear the other side before you make up your mind,

before you make any judgement at all. In practically every trial you hear in the law courts the prosecution case will sound convincing, but then once the defence case has begun you begin to ask yourself how you could possibly have been so easily persuaded. And more often than not, if you've no axe to grind, you end up in a state of indecision — which explains why juries are so reluctant to convict.

It's the same with family quarrels and fights. According to the first version the blame is all on one side; according to the second version it's all on the other side. If that happened only now and then, you might assume that one side was lying. But it happens with the most astonishing regularity, so that the inescapable conclusion is that usually both sides are exaggerating and simplifying and falsifying and exonerating themselves.

So we get this strange paradox: out of the family, the gift of God, the power for unity and tenderness and self-denial — out of this we get the destructive forces of division and strife and self-righteousness. It comes to this: that most families have some secret unhappiness, and most of those responsible deny their responsibility. The position is summed up in that doubly symbolic church in Freudenstadt: the figure on the cross beckons with outstretched arms and embraces everyone who enters, but the church is actually designed so that those entering it are divided from each other, and cannot even see each other as they approach God.

Of course the division of the sexes in the church in Freudenstadt no longer holds — not physically. Every one can sit where he or she pleases. But inside the heart the divisions remain, in Freudenstadt, here in this church, everywhere. People come into church, they come before God, to give thanks and ask for help and peace and the removal of guilt, while all the time they are both at loggerheads with their own families and convinced that they are in the right. They come forward to the outstretched arms of the figure on the cross, but they are blinkered, they have no eyes for those on their left or on their right.

And it doesn't work — not because God won't accept us, but because we are not really bringing ourselves. We're putting forward a puppet, a dummy, who represents only a part of us. It's the part we would like to be, the part we would like God to see, while that side of us that really needs grace and forgiveness — the self-righteous, indignant, embittered side of us — we leave behind and pretend doesn't exist. And then when we go out again, we wonder why we still feel uneasy, why things don't feel better, why everything isn't instantly rosy. And perhaps we begin to doubt God's love or even his existence. We all do our best to make things impossible for God.

But we can never quite succeed. Jesus said that we should forgive each other before we come to God: 'If you are offering your gift at the altar, and there remember that your brother has something against you, leave your gift there before the altar, and go: first be reconciled to your brother, and then come and offer your gift'. That always seems a kind of conscience-pricking text. But it's not a threat, it's really a promise, because what Jesus doesn't say, but what becomes apparent from his life and death, is that it is from God that we receive the power to forgive.

Left to ourselves we would never budge, never come out from behind the barriers of self-righteousness, and indignation, and wounded pride, which we erect for ourselves. We would just stay put, saying to ourselves: 'Why should I make the first move? It's the other person's fault, he started it, it's up to him to apologise, why should I be walked over?' We do anything rather than lose face, and put ourselves in the wrong.

It is only through the power of the cross that we are capable of taking a different stance. Because that is essentially what the cross is. It is God losing face, God putting himself in the wrong, God refusing to stand on his dignity by insisting that we make the first move in setting things straight: it is God letting himself be walked over. The forgiveness which the cross embodies is not just God saying, 'Forget it, let's pretend it never happened' — as if he were a sympathetic bank manager putting a line through your overdraft. The forgiveness our God offers us involves him in suffering. The beatings and insults, the spitting and the tormenting which Jesus had to endure in the lead-up to the crucifixion are not just incidental details put in to make the whole picture more dramatic. They are an integral part of the passion — they signify God being humiliated and walked over for our sake.

And it is through the power which the cross releases in our

hearts that we ourselves can forgive each other. The cross is not just an example that preachers exhort us to imitate. It is the cause of our capacity to love and to forgive.

There is a familiar Christian image of man reaching up to grasp the outstretched hand of the forgiving God. I don't think that image is apt. Certainly God stretches out his hand in forgiveness. But we respond properly, not by reaching out to him, but by holding our brother's hand.

Evangelism

$\mathcal{I}$N May 1983 four well-known ministers of the Church of Scotland presented to the General Assembly something called 'An Urgent Call to the Kirk'. Many of you will have read it. Some of you will have read it several times, because it is written in a style which is less than transparent. For those of you who have not read it, it is divided into two parts. The first part diagnoses a deep spiritual crisis in the Church of Scotland, and it identifies as the causes of this crisis the erosion of fundamental belief, the discarding of great Christian convictions, and neglect in teaching the truth of the gospel. All these are alleged to have emptied the churches. In a somewhat archaic metaphor, it is said that 'the hungry sheep look up and are not fed'. The second part of the Urgent Call prescribes the cure. The cure is mission and evangelism, based on the 'rehabilitation of evangelical belief'.

As you probably know, this document has caused a good deal of controversy. A number of people have welcomed it; a number of people have criticised it and rejected it. It can, however, be psychologically difficult to bring yourself to criticise it, because at first sight it seems so true, not to say trite. The numbers in the churches are falling, so there must be a spiritual crisis, and of course a return to the gospel must be the answer. You feel that if you disagree with the Urgent Call you automatically expose yourself to accusations of complacency or of denying the gospel, or both. But this is only a psychological difficulty, not a logical one. Because there are in the Urgent Call to the Kirk a number of blurred issues and fallacious assumptions.

Take first the word 'urgent'. Now you might think that there is good precedent for this emphasis on urgency in the teaching of Jesus himself. And several of the reactions to the Urgent Call on both sides start off by admitting without argument that the message of Christianity is always urgent. It therefore tends to be assumed that the word 'urgent' in the title to the Call gives it a kind of prophetic authority, so that you cannot ignore the Urgent Call without at the same time ignoring the proclamation of the gospel. But are we talking about the same kind of urgency?

What kind of urgency was it that Jesus proclaimed? What was it based on? In the parable of the Great Supper (Luke 14:15-24) the guests make excuses for declining their invitations. One of them has just bought a field, another some oxen: they have to go and inspect their new property. A third has just got married: of course he can't leave his new wife. None of them realises the significance of the feast to which he's been invited. Each is immersed in his own commercial or domestic affairs, and sees no further than his own nose.

What Jesus is saying is that it is the quality of the divine life, of life with God, which makes its acceptance a matter of urgency. It's not just a question of time running out — it's a question of people wasting their lives and their opportunities, getting bogged down in trivial pursuits, going up blind alleys and not realising it. Over against all this is the divine invitation: come now, it's urgent for your own sake, you're throwing away your lives, you don't understand what life really is.

Now compare that urgency, which has its roots in the divine invitation, with the urgency in the Urgent Call to the Kirk. The urgency in the Urgent Call is based explicitly on the diminishing numbers in the churches; it is a human response to a human crisis. It has nothing to do with responding to God's initiative: it is much more akin to panic in the face of human statistics. So what at first sight appeared to be in the tradition of the gospel proclamation, in fact has quite other roots. The urgency in the Urgent Call is qualitatively different from the urgency in the teaching of Jesus, so that we are at liberty to reject the one without having at the same time to reject the other.

But why should we want to reject the Urgent Call to the Kirk? The reason is that the basic assumption of the document is wrong. As I said, it diagnoses a grave spiritual crisis in the Church of Scotland, resulting from the erosion of fundamental belief. That erosion it sees in turn as the result of the decline in evangelical preaching. The cure is simply the reinstatement of evangelical preaching. Clearly, therefore, if the diagnosis is faulty so is the cure, since the diagnosis is formulated simply in terms of the absence of the cure: the disease is the absence of evangelical preaching, the cure is more evangelical preaching.

Now to my mind that diagnosis is faulty. The Urgent Call assumes that evangelical preaching means full churches. And to support that assumption it points to the simultaneous decline in evangelical preaching and in church attendance. But does that evidence of simultaneous decline in church attendance in fact support the assumption that evangelical preaching means full churches? It does not, and the fallacy in the argument is what I would call the 'frog's legs fallacy'. This is contained in the somewhat macabre story of the small boy who thought that a frog hears with its legs, and he proved his theory like this. He put a frog on the table, bent down to it, and shouted 'Jump!', whereupon the frog jumped. The boy then proceeded to cut off the frog's legs. He then bent down again and shouted 'Jump!', and not surprisingly the frog failed to jump. 'There', said the boy, 'when you cut off a frog's legs it becomes stone deaf'.

Now of course the fact that the frog no longer jumped when its legs were cut off did not at all support the boy's assumption that the frog heard with its legs. And in the same way the evidence that there has been a simultaneous decline in evangelical preaching and in church attendance does not necessarily support the assumption that evangelical preaching means full churches. It is in fact possible that evangelical preaching may cause many people to stay away from the churches. It is possible, and in the present climate it is perhaps likely.

Because the problem always facing Christians is the tension between the message of Christianity and the situation in which they find themselves. The teaching of Jesus in the New Testament is not like a book of rules which you just look up when you're faced with a difficulty. It has to be interpreted in every age and every new situation. The concepts in the New Testament which seek to express the significance of Jesus and his relationship to God and us — concepts like the Virgin Birth, and the Resurrection, and the Atonement — have to be grappled with and made sense of by each new generation. Renewal in this sense is a continual challenge to the Christian.

But renewal in the Urgent Call to the Kirk appears to mean a reversion to the old ways. What is termed 'a rehabilitation of evangelical belief' usually turns out to be simply a repetition of the message in the old forms. Take for example this expression 'the hungry sheep look up and are not fed'. One of the reasons why the hungry sheep are not fed is that the church persists in calling them hungry sheep. We wonder periodically why young people are not interested in Christianity: is it surprising when they're presented with language like this? Naturally there are some young people who will respond to it. But there are many more who revolt against it, who find in it confirmation of their suspicion that Christianity has nothing intelligible to say to them.

The church has a duty to interpret the message for the situation. It's not a new duty. The Church Fathers were doing just that, and Christians have been doing it ever since. Of course there is always the danger that you go too far: you become so involved in the situation that you forget the message and throw out the baby with the bathwater. But the alternative is not simply to refuse to throw out any bathwater at all, so that the baby drowns. That's what happens with evangelical preaching. It simply repeats the message.

Inevitably, of course, once you start trying to relate the message to the situation you take risks. Not everyone will agree with you. The only way a minister can rely on everyone agreeing with everything he says in the pulpit is either by simply repeating the language of the Bible, or by taking refuge in boring moralism. By the first, by simply repeating the message, he's not really saying anything at all: he is evading his responsibility as interpreter. By the second, by being moralistic, he is cheating: he is simply telling people what to do without telling them why. In other words, he is creating a new legalism. So the minister whom everyone agrees with is not doing his job. And the same applies to every Christian man and woman. Each of us stands alone before God.

Now certainly this is hard: it means that you can never be sure precisely where you stand; it means that there is nothing fixed and certain and immutable about the church's teaching. That is hard to live with, it's frightening, and the Urgent Call to the Kirk does not want to live with it. What it wants is fundamental belief, evangelical substance; it must be able to point to something by which the church stands or falls. It's always more comfortable to shelter behind the message and ignore the situation.

But Jesus called us to freedom, and freedom is not simply absence of constraint. It involves responsibility, the responsibility to respond individually to God's invitation, where you are, in your own situation; and in terms which make sense to you, in your own language. It has been said that this is what the temptation scene signifies, when Jesus refuses to disclose his divinity. If he had yielded to that temptation, if he had presented himself as God without disguise, in all the divine power, then there would have been no resistance; everyone would have bowed down before him. But then there would have been no freedom either, and without freedom there would have been no love. It is undoubtedly hard to live without certainty and security, it is hard to be free. But that is our calling. It is hard to be a Christian, and we have to resist attempts to make it easy.

And we have to resist such attempts even if it involves saying harsh things. That is the sad thing about the Urgent Call, that although its intention was to unite the Church of Scotland in a new concentration on the gospel the result has been rather to split the church, to harden attitudes on either side of the theological divide. It is sad, but this sort of hardening is inevitable when one type of religious temperament tries to hijack the church and insists on the exclusive correctness of its approach. Other types of religious temperament have no alternative but to resist. If the programme which they are being asked to accept is harmless then they can simply ignore it politely. But if the programme is positively wrong, if its diagnosis is mistaken and its prescription likely to make matters worse, then it must be resisted positively.

Confrontation seems to be becoming rather a dirty word nowadays. Compromise is the fashionable virtue. But compromise is not always a virtue. There are times when confrontation is the only proper course of action. And the implications of the Urgent Call to the Kirk have to be confronted and resisted.

Prayer

THE Church of Scotland recently sent a questionnaire round the churches and deduced from the answers that the great majority of churchgoers never pray, and indeed that many ministers are not in the habit of praying. This suggests to me that prayer as the subject of a sermon may not be entirely amiss.

Of course in a way it is impossible to talk about prayer. As Kierkegaard would say, it's like trying to paint the god Mars in the armour which made him invisible. It's like trying to teach someone to swim without having any access to water. It's like trying to fall in love by reading a book of poetry. Plato said about philosophy that it can't be taught, in the sense that it can't be given and received as information. Philosophy, he said, has its roots in a personal experience of mystery. The role of the teacher is not to enlighten the pupil, but to lead the pupil to discover the light within himself. So it is with prayer.

But Plato also said that teaching may be necessary to prepare the way to philosophy, and it is in this sense that talking about prayer is permissible, and indeed essential. Many of us, perhaps most of us, have a kind of mental block when it comes to prayer. We feel vaguely that it is a slightly embarrassing subject and we prefer not to talk about it. But we are conscious that in the absence of prayer there is something vital lacking in our relationship with God, in our capacity to grasp his reality.

We are like Voltaire. When he passed a religious procession in the street one day, he raised his hat to the crucifix. His companion, knowing him to be an atheist, asked him sarcastically if he now believed in God. Voltaire replied: 'We salute, but we do not speak'. That sums up the relationship many of us have with God: we salute, but we do not speak.

Or rather we cannot speak, because of this mental barrier. When I first began to study theology at university at the age of twenty-eight, I hadn't prayed since I was an adolescent. I thought that now I was a theology student I had better start again. But I went through the most terrible struggle just to get myself to say the word God as a form of address. I had gone back to university in order to search for God, to find out whether he existed, and it seemed to me that to address him as God would be to prejudice the objectivity of my search: I would be assuming the existence of what I was trying to prove.

In Somerset Maugham's novel, *Of Human Bondage*, the narrator at the age of about twenty finally shakes off the superstitions of his religious upbringing and feels himself released from what he sees as the tyranny of God. He's climbing a mountain, and when he gets to the top he is suddenly filled with an exhilarating sense of freedom, of emancipation, and he shouts: 'Thank God, I no longer believe in God!' My position at university involved a similar contradiction, only the reverse. I was saying: 'Help me, God, to believe that there is a God'. And it took a very long time and enormous effort before I could actually say the word God to God. In experiencing such a barrier I don't think I was unique, and that is why I want to say a little about prayer in an attempt to break down the barrier.

It is enough to ask one simple question: why do we pray? The easy answer is that we can't help it, at least sometimes. Again it's like love. When a prospective mother-in-law asks how her son could possibly have fallen in love with that girl, the answer is always: he couldn't help it. So with prayer. Carlyle said that prayer is the native and deepest impulse in the soul of man. Augustine put it less prosaically in the form of a prayer: 'Father, thou hast made us for thyself, and our hearts are restless until they find their rest in thee'. Prayer is spontaneous, like an artist painting, or a musician singing. You can't muzzle the person who wants to pray.

But to ask why we pray is really to raise the question of the aim, the object of prayer. At a pagan or primitive level the answer is that prayer is a cry for help. George Herbert said: 'If you want to learn how to pray, go to sea'. Prayer is a kind of Aladdin's lamp. You see this in time of war, when all the churches are full. And many of us, in spite of our twentieth century sophistication, are still primitive in our understanding of God.

But at a deeper level, the reason why we pray is to get in touch with God — in traditional terms, to have communion with God. Jesus said that there are two supreme command-ments: love God and love your neighbour as yourself. Well, the first commandment, which of course is really an invitation rather than a commandment, is fulfilled by prayer. Prayer is talking to God. It's like musicians. One reason why they play the piano is simply that they can't help playing the piano; yet their real aim is not just to satisfy an instinct but to be lifted out of themselves into a world to which only music holds the key. The object of prayer is not to make yourself heard, not to get your own way, but to be with God.

But then, there is another way of asking this question — the cynical or disillusioned way. 'Why do we pray?' then means 'What's the point of prayer, when our prayers are never answered?' Unanswered prayer is perhaps the major obstacle for many people, one that goes back to childhood disappointment. And that is the first point about unanswered prayer: very often the reason for God's silence must be our own childishness or ignorance about what we ask for. The best way of stressing this is Longfellow's remark about how disastrous it would be if all our contradictory and selfish prayers were answered. The world would be in chaos. Take the simple example of opposite sides in a war, each praying for victory. The point is that very often the true answer, the only proper answer to our prayers must be No. Look at the bit in the gospels where the mother of the two disciples asks Jesus if they can sit at his right hand in heaven, and Jesus says: 'You don't know what you're asking'.

Another example of this is someone I knew called George, who was a very earnest chap. He told me that his aunt had a friend who had a sore elbow, and one day she asked George's aunt to pray over her elbow. This was duly done and the elbow instantly cured. Now George offered that story not only as a proof of his aunt's saintliness but as a proof of the existence of God. But what kind of a god is it that allows such suffering in the world — famines, floods, cruelty, cancer — in spite of all our cries for help, and yet cures George's aunt's friend's elbow? To my mind, if you're a Christian you prefer such absurd prayers to go unanswered.

Because prayers like that are all confined within our own finite dimension, our own little world. But there is a sense in which true prayer lifts us out of this world into God's infinite world: it involves a transposition of values. The test of true prayer perhaps is that it has to be in the name of Jesus. When we say at the end of our prayers, 'For Jesus' sake', that is not just an empty formula: it is the condition of the prayer's authenticity, distinguishing it from our own little world.

Then again, our impression that prayer is unanswered may result from our ignorance, not in asking, but in listening to the answer. The answer may not be the answer we expect. Paul's thorn in the flesh is a case in point. 'Three times', he says, 'I besought the Lord about this that it should leave me, but he said to me: My grace is sufficient for you'. Or God may answer in a different way altogether, which is beyond our comprehension or our patience. When Augustine was about to leave his home in Carthage to go to Italy his mother prayed fervently that he might not go. She wanted him to become a Christian, and she thought that if he left Carthage, and her sphere of influence, he would be lost. But Augustine was resolved to go, and even as she stood praying, tears streaming down her cheeks, he set sail. Yet when he reached Italy he met Ambrose and was converted and became a Christian. So God answered his mother's prayers, even though at the time she was so sure that he had not.

And of course sometimes prayer is openly not answered. Sometimes God indicates to us that prayer is quite inappropriate. For example, in the book of Exodus, when the Israelites are fleeing from the Egyptians, God says to Moses: 'Why do you cry to me? Tell the people to go forward'. In other words, sometimes it is a question of action, and prayer cannot be a substitute. To pray then instead is to treat God as a *deus ex machina*, or the genie of the lamp.

It's scarcely a new thing, this problem of unanswered prayer. It's not something that signifies a failure or lack of faith on the part of the modern age. Actually, the Bible is full of unanswered prayer. At first sight, of course, God seems to do what he's told. There are all the miracles which Moses and Joshua and Elijah perform with his help. But in fact, over and over, God is silent. The Psalms are a catalogue of groans and cries from the depths: 'O my God, I cry by day, but thou dost not answer, and by night, but I find no rest'. And look at the scene in the garden of Gethsemane, where Jesus says: 'If it be thy will, take this cup from me. Nevertheless, not what I will, but what thou wilt'. We do not control God by prayer, we enter into his will and receive the strength to face it and to do it.

I said that when I went back to university I was searching for God, and that I found it very difficult to address God in prayer, because to pray implied that I had already found him. I think I was correct in sensing that. Prayer is commonly described and understood as seeking God's presence. But it's not that at all, it's responding to God. We tend to turn the parable of the lost sheep on its head, so that it is the sheep who are out on the mountain looking for the lost shepherd. Prayer is not a despairing shout in the darkness, it is an answer to God's call.

And here in the dimension of being found is the importance of silence in prayer. Prayer is not so much speaking to God, as listening to him. It was a gigantic struggle to bring myself to say the word God to God, but when I had said it there was nothing more to say, nothing more to learn. Prayer is not heaping up words, its content is quite immaterial. It is simply saying God to God, and letting him be God.

ℳetaphors

$\mathcal{I}$T's inevitable that we use metaphors to talk about the invisible God and our relationship with him. It's like modern science which, when it deals with things too small to be seen, has to have recourse to models; otherwise it would have to keep silent. But it's also inevitable that the models or metaphors we use will be conditioned and determined by our cultural background.

The metaphor of the shepherd and the flock of sheep was extremely common in the ancient world. The Babylonian lawgiver Hammurabi described himself as the shepherd of his people, and so did the Egyptian pharaoh. Nothing was more natural, because sheep were as much a part of everyone's life then as cars are of ours now. And in the same way Jesus in his parables always uses images from everyday life in Palestine, homely images, rural images, from the world of farming and fishing and housekeeping.

The apostle Paul, with a different background, a background of rabbinic training in the Jewish law, uses different metaphors: forensic metaphors of judgement and acquittal and punishment. And the early Christians, in their attempts to understand the significance of Jesus, generally used metaphors which made sense against the background of the Roman Empire: they talked about masters and slaves, and referred to Jesus as 'Lord'.

Now all these metaphors and models were fruitful in their own way, but there are always two dangers. The first danger is that a particular metaphor will take over and become normative. People are liable to become literalistic, particularly if as children they've had on their bedroom wall a painting of Jesus holding a shepherd's crook and carrying a lamb under his arm. They forget that religious language is only an aid to understanding, and that nobody has the final, the perfect model which explains everything.

The Buddha told a famous parable about three blind beggars who came across an elephant. The first beggar took hold of the elephant's leg and was convinced it was a tree-trunk; the second took hold of an ear, and was convinced it was the leaf of a palm-tree; the third took hold of the tail, and was convinced it was a rope. None of the three saw or grasped the concept of the whole elephant, though each thought that he had.

So, if we insist that we have found the definitive metaphor for God we're acting like one of those blind beggars, and perhaps excluding other people from the Kingdom of God. Take for example the metaphor of the fatherhood of God: what can that mean to a child whose father is an alcoholic layabout, who beats him whenever he sees him? For that child, one metaphor at least is useless and should not be insisted on.

The second danger with metaphors is that they die: they become antiquated and irrelevant and useless. But such is the power of tradition that no one realises that they are dead. Now nothing is more likely to put people off religion than the unfeeling and indiscriminate use of dead metaphors. To people who are outside the church, what does it mean to describe a minister's preaching as 'feeding hungry sheep', or to say that 'Jesus is Lord'? What can the word 'Lord' mean to men and women who live in a culture which reserves it, not for the semi-divine emperor of the whole civilised world, but for judges and peers of the realm, many of them all-too-human? And it's not just people outside the church who find this sort of language worse than useless. These models, which were supposed to lead us to God, to make intelligible our relationship with him, and in their time did so, have become instead barriers between us and God.

So, naturally, we find experiments at updating the biblical

metaphors: not just new translations, but paraphrases into a different thought-world. The Twenty-Third Psalm, for example, has been rewritten by a Japanese woman with the title 'A Psalm for Busy People'. It begins like this:

The Lord is my pace-setter, I shall not rush,
He makes me stop and rest for quiet intervals,
He provides me with images of stillness, which restore my
    serenity.
He leads me in ways of efficiency, through calmness of
    mind,
And his guidance is peace.

It's interesting that she hasn't been able to escape from the metaphor of 'Lord', but the metaphor of the shepherd and the sheep has been removed altogether, without substituting a new one. God is exalted or diminished, depending on your point of view, to a kind of principle. But, to my way of thinking, to get rid of metaphor altogether like that is to throw out the baby with the bathwater. I think our minds need some sort of model to work with: we're not content with a kind of impersonal abstraction when we come to think of God. What we need is not no metaphor, but new metaphors.

Well, there are innumerable models or metaphors we could use which might give us some insight into the nature of God and into human nature. The one I want to suggest today is the orchestra. When I was a boy I used to go during the holidays to play in a youth orchestra. And there I first became aware of the great diversity there is in the styles and personalities of conductors. We had Sir Malcolm Sargent, who was the last word in elegance and charm: when you played Elgar under Sir Malcolm Sargent you almost wished you were an Englishman. And we had Sir John Barbirolli, who always dressed like a tramp, but when he picked up his cello to show how he meant something to be played he was transformed into an angel.

But there was one conductor who commanded more respect in us than anyone else. He was Polish and he had been in the Auschwitz concentration camp during the war, and there he'd had a shoulder-blade removed, God knows under what conditions, and he could never conduct for very long at a time. But there was something in his eyes, a look of suffering overcome, a look of nobility, which when you were playing music under him inspired you to give your best in a way no mere virtuosity and panache could have done. You couldn't take your eyes off him.

At the other extreme is the story about a young conductor's first public concert. Afterwards, someone asked a member of the orchestra how the concert had gone and the musician replied: 'It was fine until some idiot looked at the conductor'. In other words the orchestra had been a self-contained unit, whose members understood one another instinctively, and who were only hampered and put out by having an inexperienced conductor to lead them.

Now you can use this model of conductor and orchestra to illumine the relationship between a minister and his congregation. It's obvious that the more successful concerts are those which have had sufficient rehearsal time, and the most successful are those where the conductor is the permanent musical director of the orchestra. Instead of being just a guest conductor who stands there waving his arms about for show, and whom the musicians pay attention to at their peril, the permanent conductor knows the strengths and idiosyncrasies of each member of the orchestra. And each member of the orchestra knows the conductor, knows what kind of music he's most at home with, knows him well enough not to misunderstand a particular gesture, and so on.

Similarly, the relationship between a minister and his congregation is an organic one, one which grows and develops and deepens over the years; and it's a mutual relationship, where each is dependent on the other and each learns from the other. Because the trouble about the metaphor of the shepherd and the sheep, if it is allowed to dominate and control our thinking, is that it places all the initiative and responsibility on the shoulders of the shepherd, and the sheep remain anonymous, indistinguishable — just sheep.

Another of the things I learnt in that orchestra was that, when you play as a member of an orchestra, your approach has to be quite different from when you're playing all alone behind closed doors. Alone, you can be as uninhibited and passionate and idiosyncratic as you please. In an orchestra, on the other hand, you have to listen to everybody else who's playing, you have to keep yourself in control; you have always to remember that you're not a soloist, but that you're making music together. It doesn't matter how glorious a tune it is you're playing, you can't throw your head back and abandon yourself: you have to express your joy or your passion or your sadness within the context of all the other members of the orchestra playing their parts as well.

That sounds as if playing in an orchestra is always a sobering experience, which curbs your instinctive individuality and exuberance. But that is not the case. Just as often, the fact that you're playing in an orchestra with other people can raise the level of your understanding of the music, and bring out of you far more than you would have thought possible playing it by yourself.

Something that always used to astonish me was this: that although the individual members of the orchestra were just what you would expect — most of them ordinary people, some of them friendly, some of them withdrawn, a few brilliant, a few unpleasant — together this random collection of people became one, they became transformed by the music they were playing, they became much greater than the sum of their parts.

And even if you particularly disliked certain individuals, when you found yourself playing music beside them their faults disappeared, and you were in harmony with each other. It is one of the closest of all intimacies between people, this making music together. When you watch a good string quartet playing, every now and then you see one of them give a little involuntary smile — it's a smile of pure delight at sharing the rhythms and melodies of the music they're making. There are few ways of getting closer to the spirit of another human being than by playing music together.

Now when we use this model to understand the life of a congregation it may seem more a model of what ought to be than of what is. Are we really brought together and lifted above ourselves when we come together into church? Do we find that when we pray together we see each other in a new light and forget each other's faults and unpleasantnesses? Do we ever smile involuntarily because we are together before God? Perhaps not, but potentially we can. Perhaps if we learn to listen to each other more, as members of an orchestra do, and make room for the parts that others have to play, then we will come closer to the spirit of God.

Because that is the third thing I learnt in that orchestra. The object of the exercise must always be to come as close as possible to the spirit of the composer, to make the music live. Often that objective can be lost to sight: with unimaginative or professionally blasé musicians the aim can simply be to pass the time pleasantly, or to earn a decent living. With the more flamboyant conductors the objective can be simply their own greater glory. The justification for the evening's music is then no longer the music itself but the applause from the audience at the end.

But the conductor, like the minister, should not be the supreme authority. He is not there to impose himself, to control things. He's there to make available his interpretation of the spirit of the composer, and to enable all the interpretations of the individual members of the orchestra to cohere, to blend together in a harmonious whole. The real musician is concerned only to realise the composer's vision, to bring it to life. And in our relationship with God, in our lives here in church or anywhere else, our purpose is to realise the spirit of God, to let it live in our lives. We don't want applause for our worship or for our lives. We are here to play God's music.

Creed and Reality

$\mathcal{T}$HERE are two advertisements currently visible in the streets of Edinburgh, which you may have seen: they are both for alcohol. One shows a bottle of Pernod and, underneath, the words 'Free the Spirit'. The other is for a certain brand of vodka, and the slogan is 'The Imperial Spirit lives'.

Now ads are generally quite an accurate indication of the intellectual and moral level of a society: of course their intention is to mould appetites, but to do so they have to conform to some extent to existing appetites. For example, I saw another ad recently which shows a succulent-looking peach and, underneath, the words 'Created by nature, perfected by man'. The words 'created by nature' don't really make sense, because of course nature is itself created, but you cannot imagine the advertisers saying 'created by God' — in a secular society that would simply make people uncomfortable. So one can deduce from a simple ad for peaches something of society's religious attitudes.

In the same way, these ads for Pernod and vodka indicate that the concept of Spirit, which has been such a potent one in the history of religion, is in our age and in the popular mind confined to bottles of alcohol. How do we free the Spirit from this confinement?

When I was a student, a friend of mine used to refer to an empty bottle of whisky as '*manes*', which is the Latin word for ghosts or, as our old Latin primer put it, 'departed spirits'. And that student pun releases us immediately from the sealed containers of our present age into the Roman world of the dead. And from there it is only a short step to stories in the Bible like the one about the witch of Endor, who conjures up the spirit of the dead Samuel so that Saul can consult him about the future. But for the Hebrew mind the idea of spirit was much less connected with death than with life. In fact the Hebrew word for spirit has the original meaning 'wind' or 'breath'; and then the breath of life, and then the life-giving principle, life itself. From there it came to be used of God who is the source of life, and then of the way in which God acts in the world, of the active presence of God either confronting people or actually in people.

In the New Testament, therefore, it's not surprising that you find the Spirit everywhere. It is said to be involved in the conception of Jesus, and it is said to descend on him at his baptism; on the day of Pentecost it comes like a mighty wind and fills the disciples; and then in his letters Paul speaks of Christians being in the Spirit and the Spirit being in Christians. And over the next three centuries the concept of the Spirit is gradually developed and filled out until finally it takes its exalted place as part of the Trinity: God the Father, God the Son, and God the Holy Spirit.

Now in starting like this from an ad for Pernod, and moving by way of the Roman underworld and the Hebrew language through the New Testament to the classic formulations of the doctrine of the Trinity, have we in any way freed the Spirit? What do we mean when we say the Apostles' Creed and come to the bit where it says: 'I believe in the Holy Spirit'?

Let me quote from the beginning of the entry on 'Holy Spirit' in a recently published dictionary of theology: 'The Holy Spirit is understood by Christians as the divine agent who brings about the Transcreation, or the culmination of human and cosmic liberation, since he perfects the Father's creative and the Son's recreative mission in history. For this reason, the Spirit is confessed as antecedently in himself the Transcreator, who is identical in being with the Father-Creator and the Son-Recreator'. That allegedly is how the Holy Spirit is 'understood by Christians'. Did you understand it?

For most of us the Spirit is anything but free. Indeed it is probably this part of the Apostles' Creed that we are most uncomfortable with, in spite of all the publicity that centres on the difficulties of the Virgin Birth and the Resurrection.

Now in tackling this problem, it is important to remember that creeds are like advertising: they follow belief, they arise out of belief, they reflect it. In the beginning, Christians said things because they believed them. And gradually the things they said were gathered together into a creed, a statement of belief. But today we have reached the stage where Christians say the words in the creed, not because they believe them but because the creed has become a test of whether or not they believe.

Creeds and dogmatic theology were originally supposed to point to the experience which gave rise to them. But what tends to happen is that they come to stand between us and real religious experience. The church's task is somehow to enable Christians to say these things again, not because they find them in the Creed but because they believe them. The task is to get behind the creeds to the experience of the Spirit which led to their formation. That is what I would call freeing the Spirit, from the sealed containers of creed and dogma.

And if we go back to the New Testament, I think that an examination of the references to the Holy Spirit in the gospels and in Paul's letters reveals that experiencing what is called the Spirit is bound up with experiencing the risen Christ. In other words, for the early Christians the conviction that Christ is not dead but alive is rooted in an awareness of the continuing presence of the spirit of Jesus. This awareness is not based on the evidence of eye-witnesses to the resurrection, nor is it a matter of deduction from the empty tomb: it comes from direct experience of the risen Christ, of his life-giving presence, or spirit.

This is what controls and challenges and comforts believers — the feeling that the spirit of Jesus is still with them, guarding them, guiding them. So that for the early Christians to say 'I believe in the Holy Spirit' would involve no dogmatic speculation or philosophical reflection; nor would it concern only an incidental aspect of their faith. It would be the natural and spontaneous way of describing the very centre of their lives — as we might say, the ground and goal of their being.

So the question is: how do we brush away all the dogmatic and speculative cobwebs of the intervening centuries and recover that original freshness for ourselves, so that we can say freely and willingly and spontaneously: 'I believe in the Holy Spirit'?

I start from the position that the Spirit which the early Christians experienced must be something which we can still experience. If it is not, then they were hoodwinked, or hoodwinked themselves, and their faith was in vain, and we may as well go home. But if the Spirit which they experienced was the Spirit of the living Christ, and if our faith is not in vain, then my first thought is that this is something which we ourselves can experience.

And my second thought is that perhaps this is something which we have already experienced. I don't mean necessarily in an explicitly religious form or framework. Take the analogy of the inspiration of a poet, or a painter, or a composer. Where does it come from, what is it? Doesn't it argue some sort of contact with a different reality from our ordinary everyday world? And this contact is not limited to the person who creates. Unless we ourselves were in principle on the same wavelength, unless we had the same contact with that other reality, we would not be moved; we would understand nothing of what we read or saw or heard. The artistic creation would be simply letters on a page, or layers of paint on a canvas, or a series of sound waves. So, to the extent that we react to the work of art, we too are inspired.

Or take the emotion of love. Of course it is possible to be cynical about love, just as it is about religion. Feuerbach, the German philosopher, argued that God is nothing but a projection of man's own wishful thinking; and in the same sort of way Stendhal, the French novelist, argued that love for another person is simply a disguise for being in love with love. When you reach a certain age, says Stendhal, you are ready for love, so that when you meet someone — it could be anyone, provided the circumstances are favourable — your feelings crystallise, as it were, around the person, and you tell yourself that you are in love.

Those of us who are more romantically inclined are reluctant to accept this theory, and want to insist that there is something special in the beloved, something unique which alone is capable of bringing out our love. But when we look at the number of people in the world, and the number of possible contacts, and the extent to which chance governs our actual contacts, we begin to wonder. Perhaps there is something in Stendhal's theory, if we reformulate it like this: when you really fall in love it's not simply the beloved you're in love with, nor is it just yourself, nor are you simply in love with love, but your relationship with the beloved has put you in touch with a different dimension, one which seems to be inaccessible in normal everyday life. It is better to be realistic: the person you love is not the only person in the world who could have introduced you to this dimension. But that doesn't really matter. What is important is the dimension itself, and the effect it has on you, and on the other person if your love is reciprocated. So in the same way as in the case of art, we can speak legitimately of being inspired by love.

As a third example, take sympathy. Now again it is possible to be cynical and reduce sympathy to nothing but fear in disguise. So it could be argued that the horror we feel when we see harrowing television pictures of disasters like volcanoes or earthquakes or famines — that horror is simply the result of projecting oneself in imagination into whatever predicament it is and recoiling in terror. And this reduction of sympathy to self-interest may contain an element of truth. But I refuse to believe that the worldwide response to the famine in Africa is simply the result of thinking: 'Wouldn't it be awful if I were in their shoes!'. There seems to be some instinct of fellow-feeling, of altruism, in most people, an instinct or drive resulting at the extreme in self-sacrifice, which is the precise opposite of the instinct for survival. If so, it is reasonable to speak of a man who lays down his life for another as inspired by something beyond himself.

Now these three forms of inspiration — inspiration by beauty, by love, and by sympathy — can be taken as analogies to experiencing the spirit of Jesus. But I would go further. The word 'inspire' means literally 'to breathe into': it is derived from the Latin word which also lies behind our word 'spirit', just as in Hebrew and Greek the words for 'spirit' mean 'breath' or 'wind' as well. What I'm saying is that there is no reason why we should not see these experiences of beauty, love and sympathy, not just as analogies to inspiration by the spirit of Jesus, but as actual instances of such inspiration. They are, if you like, intimations of divinity.

And once we have been able to identify something in our experience with the operation of the Holy Spirit, or with the presence of the living Christ, it immediately becomes possible to extend the range and to see that spirit or living presence operating elsewhere, on increasingly mundane and trivial levels. That is to say, the manifestations of the Spirit are not confined to a religious or ecclesiastical context, they are to be found everywhere in the world; they have become secularised.

In the same way, music in the course of its development in Western civilisation gradually became emancipated from the control and demands of the church and entered the real world through opera and dance. And you find the same broad progression in art and poetry, from the sacred to the profane, so that today nothing is too apparently trivial to be made the subject of a poem or painting.

Here for example are the titles of some poems in the *Oxford Book of Contemporary Verse*: Breakfast; A dentist's window; Glasgow schoolboys running backwards; Fetching cows; The shampoo; Outside the supermarket. It's not that all poetry has been trivialised; the point is that the trivial has become poetic, or rather that the poet is able to find poetic significance even in the trivial. An incident as ordinary as some Glasgow schoolboys running backwards strikes the poet as capturing something of the mystery of life.

Now an image which captures something of the mystery of life is quite a good definition of the word 'sacrament'. And the sacrament of the Lord's Supper is on one level precisely this: the disclosure of the presence of the living Christ in the most ordinary, trivial things — bread and wine, the staple diet of first century Palestine. In other words, Christianity right from the beginning contained within itself the seeds of its own secularisation.

We're accustomed, from the entrenched position of the established churches, to regard secularisation as a dirty word, the encroaching of the profane upon the sacred and the dilution of the faith. But the positive way of looking at it is the reverse: it is the freeing of the Spirit from the confines of the institution, whether physical or dogmatic, so that it can permeate the world, so that it can leaven the lump.

That is our task: to open ourselves up to the presence of Christ everywhere — in schoolboys, outside the supermarket, in fetching cows. And, having learnt how to recognise the presence of Christ, to make our own lives into the equivalent of a poem, or a painting, or a piece of music, so that other people, still trapped in the morass of the commonplace, may also learn to glimpse the sacramental realities.

$\mathcal{L}egalism$

$\mathcal{W}$HEN I was asked to come here today and talk about the present state of the Presbyterian Church of Australia, I thought initially that I would tackle yet again the issue of Fundamentalism, which seems to many people to be its chief characteristic. But it very quickly becomes boring if you keep going on about Fundamentalism, because almost always you are either preaching to the converted or talking to a brick wall. It is a pointless exercise: people either see the absurdities of the position or they don't. In fact someone has said that it takes even more of a conversion to stop being a Fundamentalist than it does to become one — and unfortunately people are rarely converted by argument.

Instead, therefore, I want to draw your attention to a different aspect of the present-day Presbyterian Church, one which is not unrelated to the question of Fundamentalism, but which is separable, and which is if anything even more alarming in its implications. I mean the conspicuous absence of the notion of the *imitatio Christi*, the imitation of Christ.

It is always a good test of the vitality and authenticity of any particular manifestation of Christianity to ask to what extent it is imitating Christ. I don't mean in the absurdly literal form which the imitation of Christ has sometimes assumed, for example the old people who so infuriated Luther when he found them playing with hoops in the street because the gospel says: 'You cannot enter the Kingdom of God unless you become as little children'. I mean rather what Luther himself called conforming to the spirit of Christ, or simply asking yourself regularly whether your response to any given situation bears any relationship to the way Jesus himself would have responded.

Sometimes of course this requires a little imagination. Harry Williams tells the story of a vicar sitting on the top deck of a London bus, wearing a clerical collar and smoking a pipe. The man in the seat behind leant forward and said angrily: 'Can you imagine Christ smoking a pipe?' To which the vicar replied: 'Can you imagine Christ sitting on the top deck of a No. 11 bus?'

But that reply was an evasion: there should be nothing impossible about imagining Christ on a No. 11 bus. Indeed, in the Middle Ages all sorts of tales and legends abounded about the *Christus redivivus* — Christ come back to earth, going round disguised as a beggar or whatever, healing the sick, showing compassion, appearing when people least expected him. And these stories captured people's imagination, and reminded them of the reality and closeness of God, and the importance of making every aspect of their lives accountable to him.

Now it has always been the formal or business side of Presbyterian church life which has made me think most anxiously about this question of the imitation of Christ. Or to be specific, the question I often ask myself is this: how would Christ react if he returned to earth and came into one of our ecclesiastical meetings?

The first time I found myself confronted with this question was shortly after I became a minister, when I attended the General Assembly of the Church of Scotland in Edinburgh. The General Assembly in Scotland is marked by considerably more pomp and circumstance than your equivalent here. It begins on a Sunday with a service in St. Giles' Cathedral, with innumerable processions of the good and great, festooned in scarlet robes, gold jackets, white gowns, wigs, medals and chains — not the chains of servitude but the chains of office. And it's the same story throughout the Assembly itself, with the macer, and the purse-bearers, and the Lord High

Commissioner and his ladies, and all the dress-ups, and the reserved seats for ex-Moderators, the stars of former years. It's all historically understandable of course, and if you like pageantry it's colourful and even exciting.

But I'm afraid I found myself asking: does it have any place in Christianity? What have all these dignified processions and gorgeous costumes to do with the naked Christ hanging on a cross? What if Jesus came back during Assembly week, what if he were sitting in the aisle watching them all file past with measured tread — would they look so sleek and self-satisfied then? Would they have such an air of authority?

Things are slightly more democratic in the Presbyterian Church of Australia. But what would happen at a Presbytery meeting or a General Assembly meeting if Christ were to come back, *Christus redivivus* as in the old medieval legends — what would happen if he suddenly appeared in our midst? I'll tell you what I think would happen. Someone would get up and brandish a copy of the Code of Procedure and shout that there was nothing in it which gave Christ any right to address the meeting. And there would be a motion on it, and a counter-motion, and several amendments, and the odd point of order, and the Church would be divided down the middle, and Christ would remain unheard.

What I'm saying is that there is a new legalism abroad in the Church, which is threatening to take control and in the process extinguish the spirit of Christ. I have no difficulty in envisaging Christ sitting on the top deck of a London bus; but I cannot by the wildest stretch of my imagination see him waving a copy of the Code of Procedure. Because it was precisely this stranglehold of law, of rules and regulations, which Christ came to free us from.

The trouble about law is that it operates by defining things. It sets limits, it tells us what we can and cannot do. And when you define something you automatically exclude something else — by definition: if you set limits, then you inevitably place something outside these limits. And the Judaism of Jesus's time, with the best will in the world, tried to apply this kind of thinking to man's relationship with God. It tried to capture, to put down on paper, every nuance of that relationship, so that it ended up with literally hundreds of rules and regulations covering every conceivable aspect of daily life. What it failed to realise was that the more you define, the more you exclude: the more detailed you become in your insistence on obedience, the more you find that you haven't taken into account.

And on to this nit-picking, gnat-straining scene Jesus erupted, telling people about a different kind of God altogether, a God who doesn't demand obedience above all else, who isn't interested in our pathetic little sins; a God of love, a God who loves us and wants our love in return. And of course love has nothing at all in common with law. Love operates in quite a different way: it doesn't define and therefore exclude — it embraces, it has no limits. Its mode of address is not 'You miserable sinner, do not do this or that', but 'Come to me, all you who are heavy-laden, and I will give you rest'. Or as Paul puts it: 'For freedom Christ has set us free'.

Christianity is a religion of freedom: that is what love is, it liberates, it opens up, it removes barriers, it enables us to become different people. Now I have spoken about Christian freedom before and it has got me into trouble, because people think I mean something like licence or antinomianism. They think that this kind of freedom is a mirage, or a snare and a delusion; they think in fact that it is a soft option, which fails to take seriously enough the holiness of God, the divine will, the divine law.

But that is a misunderstanding: there is nothing soft about the freedom I have in mind, nothing easy about it. In fact it is a terrifying freedom, and in the face of it many of us react like old lags, who whenever they are released from prison commit another crime, not because they are incurably wicked, but because they are horrified at the prospect of being free and responsible for their own lives: they miss the security, the safety of the prison walls. And perhaps it is exactly this that lies behind the new legalism in the Church: it is fear of Christian freedom, it is fear of God's love. It's always much easier to shelter behind the rigid and unyielding certainties of the Code of Procedure.

Obedience, you see, comes much more naturally to human beings than love or freedom. Anyone can obey — that's nothing. But to love! That requires talent, inspiration — literally. And to be free — that's the last thing people want, however much they pay lip-service to the idea. In fact they generally put to death those who offer them freedom. One thinks of Socrates, whom they accused of corrupting the morals of the young; one thinks of Jesus, whom they accused of blasphemy; one thinks of all those so-called heretics who died at the hands of the Spanish Inquisition.

There is a story in Dostoevsky about Christ coming back to earth during the time of the Spanish Inquisition. It's called 'The Legend of the Grand Inquisitor', and in it Christ appears in Seville the day after a hundred heretics have been burned at the stake in a great *auto-da-fe*. He appears as he did during his lifetime, and the crowds recognise him at once, and he heals the sick. At the steps of the cathedral he meets a funeral procession for a little girl, and he has compassion on the mother and brings the child back to life. And just at that moment the Grand Inquisitor is passing and sees what has happened and orders his guards to arrest Christ and throw him into prison. And that night the Grand Inquisitor, an old man who has served the Church throughout his long life, visits Christ in the dungeons and talks to him.

It is in fact a monologue, because Christ remains silent throughout. And the Grand Inquisitor tells Christ that he will have him burned at the stake the next day as the worst of heretics, because he has come back to undo the work of the Church.

The point is that the Grand Inquisitor understands perfectly well that Christ came originally to offer freedom to mankind: he wanted man's free, unforced love, in place of the ancient rigid law. This lies at the heart of the temptation scene in the desert: if Christ had agreed to turn the stones into bread, he would have had no difficulty in persuading men to follow him — people everywhere would have flocked to him. But Jesus rejected that option — he resisted the temptation. He refused to coerce mankind, he didn't want blind obedience: he preferred freedom — without freedom it would all be worthless.

But, says the Grand Inquisitor, that was a mistake. Man doesn't want freedom, he wants simply to be happy; and the only way to make him happy is to deprive him of his freedom. Man's greatest need is to find someone to whom he can hand over this gift of freedom as quickly as possible, and that, says the Grand Inquisitor, is where the Church stepped in. The Church, not Christ, had man's happiness in mind; the Church had the good sense to correct Christ's work, to take away man's freedom, and to give him the bread he asked for. What mankind craves is simply someone to obey.

As I said, throughout this monologue Christ remains silent. When the Grand Inquisitor has finished he waits for a reply — he longs for Christ to say something, however bitter, however terrible. But suddenly Christ gets up and comes over to the old man and softly kisses him on his aged, bloodless lips. That is all his answer. The old man shudders. He goes to the door, opens it, and says to the Prisoner: 'Go, and come no more'. And he lets him out into the dark alleys of the town: the Prisoner goes away.

Now the Legend of the Grand Inquisitor has very subtle overtones. The old man is a figure of tragic, indeed heroic, proportions, because his driving force is his love of mankind. His secret is really that he doesn't believe in God, but he keeps it a secret. His whole life is a deception, for the sake of mankind's happiness. That is his saving grace: I think that if such a figure had really existed, he would probably have ended up in Paradise, as it were in spite of himself.

The question is, though, whether these attenuating circumstances apply to those in the Presbyterian Church of Australia who insist on removing people's freedom and substituting for it blind obedience. It may be that they do apply: it may be that there is a real anxiety for the well-being of the average man and woman in the pew, and the feeling that they have to be protected from the dangers of free and uninhibited inquiry. It may be that behind all this apparent obscurantism there does lie a genuine pastoral concern. It is possible. It is not a good idea to assume the worst of one's opponents, particularly one's theological opponents: the *odium theologicum*, theological hatred, is all too ready to rear its head, and it has already done untold damage in the history of the Presbyterian Church of Australia.

But I would say this: that even if their motives are above suspicion, even if they are pure as the driven snow, I think they are wrong. I think that freedom is the true criterion of Christianity. Obedience is a concept which is essentially alien to it. And legalism is a creeping, insidious thing, the very antithesis of Christian freedom: it represents the correcting of Christ's work.

Let us not try to correct Christ's work, as the Grand Inquisitor did, however good our motives. Let us simply accept the grace of God, the freedom which he has given us in Christ.

Myth

ANTAEUS was a character in Greek mythology whom it was very difficult to get the better of in a fight, because his mother was the Earth, and every time you knocked him down he received renewed energy from contact with the ground and came back for more. Eventually Hercules defeated him by lifting him above his head and chucking him over a cliff into the sea.

But Antaeus is also a brand of men's deodorant. There is an ad for it on television at the moment, showing a muscle-bound he-man lifting a huge bottle of deodorant above his head, and this is accompanied by one of those epic voices saying: 'Antaeus — the myth becomes a man'.

The myth becomes a man. In other words, the reverse of the process which led to the myth of Antaeus in the first place, because the characteristic thing about Greek mythology is that its gods and goddesses are really just human beings blown up into mythical proportions, with all the appetites, defects, and unpleasantness of ordinary men and women.

It is probable that something similar happened in the case of Isaiah's prophecy: 'For unto us a child is born, to us a son is given; and the government will be upon his shoulder, and his name will be called "Wonderful Counsellor, Mighty God, Everlasting Father, Prince of Peace".' The language has a great deal in common with certain psalms which celebrated the enthronement of the king in ancient Israel, and some scholars think that Isaiah has taken what was originally an enthronement psalm and applied it to an ideal king of the future. In course of time, particularly after the Exile when the fortunes of Israel were at their lowest, it became more and more common for the Jews to pin their hopes on this future king, who came to be referred to as the Messiah, the Lord's anointed, or in Greek, Christos, the Christ. Indeed by New Testament times this ideal figure who would save Israel had acquired several other titles in advance: son of God, son of Man, servant of the Lord, and so on.

Now it seems that Jesus, whatever he may have thought of himself, did not actually claim to be the Messiah. But after his death the first Christians were convinced that he had been, and so it was inevitable that all the available messianic titles which were, so to speak, in the air, should be applied to him. Not all at once, of course, but different ones at different times and by different groups of Christians; and later all these titles were gathered together in the documents which came to be known as the New Testament, together with many other descriptions of Jesus, such as redeemer, pre-existent one, first born of all creation, logos or word made flesh.

All these were attempts, like the story of the Virgin Birth, to express the significance of Jesus. And in the end they were formally enshrined in the Creeds, which speak of Jesus as the God-man, the union of the divine and the human, the co-existence of two natures in one person. The man had finally become a myth.

The distinction between the two, between the man and the myth, is captured in an apocryphal version of the scene at Caesarea Philippi. According to this version, when Jesus asked the disciples 'Whom do you say that I am?' the disciples replied in the words of the fourth century Nicene Creed: 'You are the Lord Jesus Christ, the only begotten son of God, begotten of your Father before all worlds, God of God, Light of Light, Very God of Very God, begotten, not made, being of one substance with the Father, by whom all things were made, who for us men, and for our salvation, came down from heaven, and was incarnate by the Holy Ghost of the Virgin Mary, and was made man...' And Jesus said: 'WHAT???!!!'

In our own century an enormous amount of labour has been expended on examining each of these titles and descriptions of Jesus, their development in Jewish or Hellenistic usage, the history of their application to Jesus, and the different shades of meaning in the various New Testament writers. And vast quantities of grey matter have been used up in the effort to comprehend the logic of the early Christian theories about what happened in Jesus: how, as the hymn puts it, 'the Word became incarnate, and yet remained on high'.

And it's difficult not to smile at all this historical research and critical acumen being applied to what are so obviously metaphors, drawn from the available stock of messianic expectations and philosophical ideas; because since these metaphors are so clearly time-bound and culturally conditioned there is no earthly reason why we should be obliged to retain them, any more than there is any reason why we should bind ourselves to the process by which men became gods in Greek mythology.

When you get a Christmas cracker you're not as a rule particularly interested in the cracker itself: you pull it, and find out what's inside, and throw the wrapper away. But last week I read in the newspaper about certain very expensive crackers, costing about $100 each, which have extremely ornate wrappers, gold paper encrusted with imitation pearls and so on, and inside a bag of sweets or a plastic toy. So that what you're really paying for, if you're silly enough to buy them, is the wrapper.

Now that's the kind of inversion of values you have when all the emphasis is placed on the titles in the New Testament — Christ, logos, son of God, pre-existent one, etc. And that's the kind of inversion of values you have when you're expected to recite the Creeds without having any experience of what lies behind them and gave rise to them. Christianity is then a kind of showcase religion, where the wrappings are more important than what's inside.

We mustn't feel shackled by the titles in the New Testament. There's nothing to stop us rejecting them if they mean nothing to us, and nothing to stop us creating new ones which do mean something. After all, we are in exactly the same position in relation to God and Jesus as these early Christians were. They responded in terms of their intuitions and background, and the result was the New Testament. We must respond too, in terms of our intuitions and our background, otherwise we are only Christians at second-hand; window-shopping Christians, dazzled by a display of expensive and exciting-looking crackers, but with no very clear idea of what they might contain, and with a sneaking, unspoken suspicion that they might contain nothing at all.

But there has also been a trend in our age in precisely the opposite direction; that is, in the direction of tearing off everything that could conceivably be called wrapping, in order to arrive at the gift inside. This process is known as demythologising — clearing the historical site on which the edifice of myth has been erected.

Now myth in this sense does not mean simply something which is untrue, as it tends to do in our modern everyday usage — for instance when we say: 'It's a myth that the government will cut the rate of income tax next year'. There it simply means an unfounded rumour. But when scholars say that the Bible contains myths they mean stories which are not factually and historically true, but which nevertheless say something which is true.

A good example is the creation myth right at the beginning of the Bible, which most people nowadays regard not as a scientifically accurate account of what actually happened, but as a story which discloses the true relationship between God and the world, and between God and us, and between us and the world.

And this business of demythologising is something which we are duty-bound to engage in, once we have begun to realise that the New Testament does contain such a thing as myth. But it is a dangerous business, because if the result of our endeavours is simply that the myth becomes a man then we have cheated. Our aim was to make Christianity intelligible, but it turns out that we have diluted it into something insignificant.

What drove the early Christians to their extreme metaphors and their bewildering speculations about pre-existence and so on, was their conviction that Jesus was both human and divine, both related to us and related to God. Nothing would have been easier than to deny the divinity, or to deny the humanity of Jesus. Either way the difficulties would have been removed.

But either way something vital would have been lost.

It's the same today. We can turn Jesus with the greatest of ease into a supremely good man, the greatest, the purest, the kindest who has ever lived. And as soon as we do that he ceases to be of any interest to us. The very name Jesus means 'he saves', and no mere man, whoever he is, will save us, because it is precisely our humanity that we require to be saved from.

So the progression from myth into man might work for deodorants, but it doesn't work for Christianity. What we have to do, once we have demythologised, once we have recognised the New Testament myths for what they are, is to re-mythologise: in other words to find new myths, new vehicles for expressing against a twentieth century background our sense of the significance of Jesus. And it is up to each of us to find some such myth, some way of making sense of where we stand in relation to God, some way of responding to him.

Take the analogy of music. In the world of music there are people called musicologists, who work away at the historical background to a piece of music. They try to find the version closest to the original manuscript, they try to discover as nearly as possible what the composer's intentions were, and then they produce an edition of the piece of music which is as authentic as possible. But that's not the end of the process. The music now has to be played before it can, properly speaking, exist. There has to be a fusion of two minds, the mind of the composer and the mind of the performer, before the music comes to life.

Now applying that analogy to Christianity, the New Testament scholar is the equivalent of the musicologist. The scholar does the spadework, studying the background and the documents, identifying the later additions and embellishments to the tradition and the myths and legends which have grown up, and trying to uncover the historical Jesus, to whom the various documents in the New Testament are so many responses. Because Jesus himself is the equivalent in this analogy to the piece of music. And the historical Jesus, just like the piece of music, has no full reality taken in a vacuum.

There is a well-known German professor of theology who is fond of saying in his lectures: 'God does not exist, he happens'. Like most theological statements it sounds better in German, but what he means is that God is not an abstraction which one can contemplate in a detached, philosophical sort of way: God is really God only when he encounters us, when he comes to meet us and engages us. And he does that in Christ. So in the same way Jesus Christ does not exist, he happens. As with the piece of music, it is only when we respond to him that we can fully affirm his reality.

And we are all called to respond to him, each in our own way, just as no two performances of the same piece of music are ever identical. The way I respond to God in Jesus is my myth: what I make of my life, how I turn my whole character, my attitudes, my career, my ambitions, into the story of my response to Jesus. That is my personal, individual myth, which, though it may be outwardly unimpressive, inconsistent, even meaningless, even ludicrous, may yet contain enough truth for it to be said that my existence has been justified.

Public Opinion

$\mathcal{I}$'VE been reading *Aesop's Fables*, and there is one which concerns a father, a son, and a donkey. The donkey was tired one day, and the father and son were walking along beside it when they heard a passer-by saying: 'What a waste of a donkey — why don't the stupid people get on its back?' So they did, and a little further on they heard someone else say: 'What cruelty to a dumb beast — why don't they get off and stop torturing it?' So they got off and slung the donkey on a pole and carried it between them; and after a little while they went over a bridge and the donkey fell off into the river and was drowned. The moral presumably is that you should pay no attention to what other people say.

Which, in our age of conformity, is a tall order. We probably pay more attention to what other people say than ever before, for the very good reason that we know more clearly what it is they do say. Television and the newspapers not only tell us what happens, they tell us what other people think about what happens, and therefore what we think we ought to think. They mould opinion.

So that you get the ironic situation that in an age of so-called free-thinking there are probably as many orthodoxies and sacred cows as there ever were in less enlightened ages. The great sin nowadays is to flout received opinion. To have unorthodox views on South Africa, for example, is to invite social ostracism at the least. There are anonymous pickets everywhere making sure that the orthodox view prevails. In a way, of course, this is relaxing: we don't need to feel responsible for what we think, if it's simply what everyone else thinks. We can shelter behind the next person: if everyone else is shouting 'Crucify him!', then it can't be our fault. Having an independent mind, on the other hand, can be very demanding.

Christianity started off bravely in this respect, because it began as a minority movement: for the first three hundred years of its existence it was synonymous with independence of mind. It was regarded by the authorities of the Roman Empire as subversive; it was the antithesis of public opinion. But then with Constantine it became the official religion of the Empire: it was no longer eccentric, the mark of the outsider. The great outsiders now were the heretics, those who dared to question the accepted beliefs of orthodoxy. Christianity had become received opinion.

And so, to some extent, it remains. Oddly enough, religious conformity is often expected more by those outside the church than by those within it. When it was proposed recently that a convicted murderer should be licensed as a Church of Scotland minister it was surprising, and in a way amusing, to see the indignation expressed by people who don't regard themselves as Christians, and who never darken a church door. Christians are presumed to conform to what people think and expect.

I don't need to tell you how dangerous this can be: how conformity to the spirit of the age can stifle the spirit of God and lead to a secondhand religion, a religion of the minimum, of what everyone can agree to. The great protestant principle, which is more honoured in the breach even in the protestant churches, is that everyone stands alone before God. We can never say to God: 'I was only obeying orders'; or 'I believe this because other people do'; or 'I can't do this because of what people might say'. If your relationship with God has to be filtered through other people's experiences, if it can only be a sort of common denominator of what everyone else believes, then you are worshipping an idol: you are a slave to public opinion and you have no Christian freedom.

Religion is like the donkey in the fable. It should be your servant and your partner. You must not abuse it by always riding it into the ground; nor fail to make proper use of it by always walking along at its side; nor distort its proper character by carrying it on your back, so that you become its servant. Religion can very easily become abused or neglected or distorted, if you listen only to what other people say.

And this applies not just to what our contemporaries say but also, and perhaps to a greater extent, to what people have said in the past. I'm talking about tradition, the inert mass of received opinion which remains anchored in the past but which is always threatening to squeeze the life out of us with its dead weight. It's a more powerful idol, this, because at first sight it seems indistinguishable from the true God. And it takes a certain amount of courage and experience to separate this idol from the true God.

I can illustrate the dilemma like this. The Bishop of Durham first hit the headlines by making known his unorthodox views on the Virgin Birth and the Resurrection, neither of which he accepts in its literal form. Now this has caused a great outcry in some sections of the Church of England. Many people are saying that they are confused and perplexed now that they no longer have the traditions of a lifetime to hold on to. And one sympathises.

But then look at the other side. Earlier this year there was a controversial series of programmes on television which concentrated on the findings of biblical scholars in the last hundred years. And there was an outcry then among church members, but this time against the ministers for having kept people in the dark about these developments. There seemed to have been a conspiracy of silence. Ministers seemed to have been operating with a double standard: it was all right to be critical in the theological colleges, but not in front of the children — in this case the congregations.

Now of course together these two conflicting responses on the part of church members simply go to show that the minister can't win. We all knew that. But the response of the first group, the anger against churchmen daring to question tradition, is I think largely based on fear: fear that the certainties of faith are being undermined and, deeper down, fear that in the searchlight of criticism God will be discovered to be an idol.

In fact, ironically, in their haste to affirm the fixed validity of the tradition, such people deny the reality of the resurrection. Because the resurrection means that there is nothing fixed about Christianity. There is nothing rigid, nothing demonstrable, nothing objective which you can point to and say: 'This is Christianity: believe this and you are a Christian, do this and you are a Christian'.

Someone once asked me to say in one sentence why Jesus came. I thought for a minute of a clever way of epitomising two thousand years of soul-searching and imagination in a single pithy sentence. But then it occurred to me, no. Why should I? Why should it be possible? If it were possible, then it would make a mockery of Jesus. It would mean that this single sentence was as important as his entire life and death. It would mean that we were making a system of God and his activity. It would mean that we were worshipping a neat little idol of our own making, instead of the living God.

Being a Christian means being open to the living God. Christianity is openness: a refusal to let yourself be controlled, or enslaved, whether by public opinion or by the weight of tradition. Jesus said: 'If you continue in my word, you are truly my disciple, and you will know the truth, and the truth will set you free'. Free, that is, from idols of any description, free from each other and from the past: free to open ourselves to God and to worship him in spirit and in truth.

Of course that doesn't mean that we must live in a spiritual vacuum, and ignore completely what other people think and throw all tradition out of the window. We have much to learn from other people and from the past. But we must never be a slave to either. They should always be a means to an end, channels leading us to God, not irresistible tides carrying us on to the rocks.

The Christian is really like the artist. Artists have to listen, at least in their formative years, to what other people say, in order to understand how other eyes see their work; they have to study the past in order to find out where they are and how best to express what is in inside them. But if they let themselves be controlled either by other people or by the past they will be very indifferent artists.

So it is with the Christian. Of course you must test your vocation — your understanding of God's will for you — against the understanding of the community of believers; and you must test it against the doctrines and traditions of the church. But it always remains your vocation, God's will for you. And if after due consideration you come to the conclusion that it conflicts with what other people think, or with the traditional way of understanding things divine — then so be it. It is God you must listen to, because in Christ you have been set free — precisely in order to listen to God.

$\mathscr{B}arriers$

$\mathcal{T}$HERE are many different kinds of barrier between us and God. The most obvious kind is the intellectual, which includes innumerable misunderstandings about God; for example, that God wants obedience rather than love, or that sin is anything you like doing, or that the Bible is a book of rules like a statute-book, or that God only reveals himself in visions. But today I want to say something about another kind of barrier, the kind which has its roots in the way we look at the world, in our life-style, in our self-understanding. In fact, this kind is not so much a barrier *between* us and God: it's rather that we ourselves *constitute* the barrier. The barrier is the self.

I shall take three aspects of this obstructive self. First of all, self-assertion. About a month ago my wife and I went to a party. It was a very highbrow party; most of the people there were academics, and to judge by their own claims there can never have been such a gathering of brilliant minds under one roof. The first person I spoke to treated me to a selection from the reviews of his latest book. And words like 'pioneering', 'inspired' and 'outstanding' came up repeatedly. The next guest I was introduced to had a different method of drawing attention to himself: he shone at the expense of other people. He entertained me for quarter of an hour by being extremely malicious about a rival professor, and of course no one can be more amusingly malicious than an academic about a rival. Then there was a woman whom we hadn't seen for about ten years, and she gave us an exhaustive account of her career since then, telling us that she was really at the pinnacle of her profession and had astounded everyone by her talents and her flair.

My wife said afterwards that she had never met so many achievers. I thought that was rather kindly put. My word would have been megalomaniacs. And it occurred to me to wonder what would have happened if the old Russian legend had come true that night, about Christ coming back to earth again in disguise. What if Christ had been a guest at that party? Would anyone have recognised him, would anyone even have listened to him — or would they all have been too busy telling him about the reviews of their latest book?

Perhaps not surprisingly, that party induced in me a feeling of nausea so that I had to leave early. I was actually starting some sort of bug, and I felt very faint, so I left in a hurry before my wife and waited for her outside in the street. I felt so faint that I had to sit down, and the only place to sit was on the edge of the pavement. So there I sat in the rain, with my tie undone and my hair dishevelled and my face flushed. And while I waited several cars went past, and the occupants of each car looked out at me with expressions of intense disgust and disapproval, obviously under the impression that I was hopelessly drunk.

I tell this story partly in case any of the people in those cars came from this area of the city and recognised me, in which case you now have the true version; but really I tell it because it illustrates the second aspect of the obstructive self — selfrighteousness. It is so easy for prejudice, preconceptions, selfrighteousness to stand in the way of compassion. And again I ask the question: what if the Russian legend came true and it was Christ sitting there on the edge of the pavement, helpless, unwell, in need? How many of us would look at him with disgust and dismiss him as just another drunkard or drug-addict, someone letting down the side?

And the third aspect of the obstructive self is self-satisfaction. Someone asked me recently, and rather aggressively, why it was necessary ever to sing new and unfamiliar hymns, indeed why it was necessary even to have new hymn-books. What was wrong with all the old favourites? She was, she told me —

rather unnecessarily — a traditionalist. Well, I tried gently (but not, I fear, with much success) to point out to her that those favourite old hymns which she regarded with such firm approval were themselves new once — mostly in the middle of the nineteenth century — and that her nineteenth century counterparts had probably resisted *their* introduction with equally indignant zeal. Indeed in many churches in Scotland even the installation of an organ met with fierce hostility.

What then is a traditionalist? At what point does tradition become crystallised and therefore sacrosanct? Is it in 1615 with the publication of the *Scottish Psalter*, or in 1898 when the original edition of the *Church Hymnary* appeared, or in 1927 when the predecessor of our current hymn-book was put together? And if any of these why?

The truth is that Christianity — not just hymns and hymn-tunes, but Christianity in the sense of our whole response to the person of Christ — Christianity in this total sense has been changing ever since its inception. And to rest satisfied with any particular form of response and insist on its permanent validity — even for yourself, far less for other people — is a betrayal of the spirit of Christianity and a denial that Christ still lives and still comes.

For a third time I ask the question: what if the Russian legend came true and Christ returned to earth and stood up here in this church and announced 'a new song to the Lord'? How many of us would close our hymn-books in irritation and mutter to our neighbour that we didn't know the tune and had no intention of learning it?

There is a cautionary tale which is relevant here, concerning a well-known Scottish minister, Harry Whitley, who became minister of St. Giles' Cathedral in Edinburgh. In his autobiography, which he calls 'Laughter in Heaven', he tells a story about his first parish in the 1930s, when he was green and unused to the ways of the world. There was a bell in the church tower, a very fine bell, very old; but during the First War a bomb had fallen nearby and the force of the explosion had knocked the bell off-centre, so that instead of a fine, sonorous clang it produced — and had produced for the past twenty years — a pathetic, dull thud.

Well, Harry Whitley thought that this was a miserable waste

of a fine asset, but he knew that the church didn't have much money. So after he had been there for about six months he arranged privately for a friend who was expert in these things to rehang the bell, and the next Sunday it rang out clear and loud before the service.

But immediately after the service, when Harry Whitley had come down from the pulpit and gone into the vestry, an angry session clerk burst in, followed by the rest of the elders, and shouted: 'What have you done to our bell?' They were furious that it was no longer producing the customary clunk; they were deaf to any considerations of aesthetics, or to the inspiring effect a real chime might have on the neighbourhood; their only concern was the preservation of what they were accustomed to, even if it was a grotesque travesty.

We do make things very difficult for God, and I imagine that there are tears in heaven as well as laughter when we turn ourselves into barriers like this. A much better model for the Christian is the artist whom Don Quixote came across working on a canvas. 'What is it?', asked Don Quixote. 'Whatever it turns out to be', replied the artist. That is the proper Christian attitude to the future and to the self. Self-assertion, self-righteousness, self-satisfaction — all evaporate if we allow God to work on us, and if we let ourselves become whatever we turn out to be.

Change

'To live is to change', said Cardinal Newman, 'and to be perfect is to have changed often'. Very shortly after I came here I was interviewed by two members of the Sydney Presbytery for the magazine of the Presbyterian Church of Australia, and in reply to one of their questions I quoted that remark of Cardinal Newman. In due course an account of the interview was printed, and in it Newman was misquoted as follows: 'To live is to change, and to be perfect is to have changed not'. I must assume that this was a mistake, but if so it was a Freudian mistake, because the misquotation exactly captures the distinguishing mark of the Fundamentalism which is beginning to permeate the Presbyterian Church of Australia. To the Fundamentalist way of thinking, to be perfect is to have changed not.

Now some of you may think that it would be a good thing if I showed some sign of changing and stopped hitting out constantly at Fundamentalism. There are two reasons why I am unlikely to change in that regard.

The first is that I regard Fundamentalism as an exceedingly dangerous phenomenon. Individually, of course, its exponents can scarcely be said to constitute a threat to anything, but collectively they stand for something sinister, and something which is very much on the increase in our world. It is not confined to the Presbyterian Church, or to Christianity, or even to religion.

Its final form is totalitarianism: an Orwellian nightmare of thought-police and tyranny. Because what we are faced with is not just a slightly farcical form of obscurantism, devoid of intellectual respectability; and not just a pathetic desire for power and authority which would otherwise be inaccessible. What we are really talking about is a threat on a massive scale to individuality and freedom and growth. A threat in fact to the possibility of change, because without change you cannot have individuality, or freedom, or growth.

And the second reason why I am unlikely to stop taking pot shots at Fundamentalism whenever I have the chance, is that not only is it dangerous in itself, it is inimical to Christianity. The two are opposites: Fundamentalism is the perversion of Christianity, and as such it is not only dangerous, it is demonic.

Because Christianity essentially is a matter of individuality, freedom and growth, it is essentially a matter of change. 'To live is to change, and to be perfect is to have changed often'. Newman of course, having changed publicly and dramatically several times in his life, may simply have been making a virtue of necessity. But his maxim captures the spirit of Christianity, it captures the central importance to Christianity of the idea of risk.

There is nothing in the least cautious or pusillanimous about Christianity. It might in fact be said to be the punter's religion. When I was young, or at least younger, I was very influenced by what is known as Pascal's wager. Pascal was a French mathematician and philosopher of the seventeenth century, and one of the few thinkers in the past two thousand years who have been able both to glimpse and to articulate the heart of Christianity.

It was Pascal who made the distinction between the god of the philosophers on the one hand — a kind of abstraction who might or might not be necessary to a philosophical understanding of the world — and on the other the God of Abraham, Isaac and Jacob, the God who can only be known in practice, in reality, in person.

And Pascal described our predicament more or less like this: either God exists or he doesn't exist. If he doesn't exist, then life is meaningless and it doesn't really matter what we do. But if he does exist, then it is worth doing anything in order to find him and know him. In other words we should be prepared to sacrifice everything and take any risk, because in a sense we can't lose: if we do find him, then life will be marvellous; if we don't, then life would have been miserable anyway.

That is Pascal's wager. Not perhaps mathematically water-tight, but then Christianity is not a mathematical religion. Because in fact Pascal's wager is simply a philosophical restatement of the parable of the merchant who sells everything he has to buy the one pearl of great price. The difference is that Pascal is simply putting the alternatives, whereas the parable demands action. Risk is not something you talk about: it is something you do.

This is demonstrated most succinctly in the story about the young man who was sitting an entrance exam for Cambridge University. There was only one question in the exam paper, and it consisted of only three words: 'What is risk?' The young man's answer consisted of only two words: 'This is'. I'm glad to say that he passed the exam and went on to do great things.

It reminds me of another exam story, which I'm afraid I don't remember very clearly, but I think it involved engineering, and the question was how would you determine the height of a skyscraper using a barometer. There was presumably a conventional answer to this question, but one particularly brilliant student scorned to give the conventional answer: instead he amused himself by listing sixty-seven different ways of finding the height of the building, each more unexpected than the last. I only remember two of them. One was to go to the top of the skyscraper and lower the barometer to the ground at the end of a piece of string, which could then be measured. The other was to find the caretaker and offer him the barometer in exchange for divulging the height of the building.

Now this approach obviously involved an element of risk as well. There was always the possibility that the examiners would have a sense-of-humour failure, or turn out to be the academic equivalent of the Fundamentalists, who see the textbook answer as the only possibility. But the student's answers were also an exercise in what is called lateral thinking. The natural habitat of lateral thinking is of course the business or management world: it is a fashionable problem-solving tool. But it is also connected with something crucial in Christianity.

When the New Testament talks about repentance, it doesn't simply mean saying you're sorry for past faults and being determined to turn over a new leaf in the future. The Greek word for repentance means a change of mind, and the Hebrew word means a turning round. One of the distinctive things about the teaching of Jesus is that it presents a dramatic change of values: the first shall be last and the last first. God never does what you expect; his ways are not man's ways, he is full of surprises. In order to respond to this God, you have to be prepared to shift the centre of gravity of your thinking, you have to change your mind in a much more profound sense than simply reprogramming it, you have to be open to entirely new possibilities.

Take, for example, the question of obedience. The Judaism of the first century was in practice centred on obedience. Man's relationship to God was expressed in terms of commandments and obedience to commandments. Of course it wasn't quite as monochrome and depressing as the traditional caricature has made out. Modern scholars have shown that there was room for the ideas of love and forgiveness as well; the pious Jew rejoiced in the commandments — they were a sign of God's love — and he rejoiced in obeying them. But his religion was still founded on law and obedience to law, and the thing about law and obedience is that they confine rather than liberate. They tend to stunt growth, and imprison the individual, and constrict freedom. And law is inherently resistant to change.

Now Jesus came into this stifling atmosphere like a cyclone. He didn't lay down more laws or different laws, he didn't demand even greater obedience. He came, as Paul says, to set us free. He came to tell us to change our minds — about God. He told parables, stories about a God who thinks quite differently from us, who doesn't demand things from us but wants to give us things — ultimately himself, if we can only bring ourselves to take the risk of listening to him, and opening ourselves up to him.

The eighth chapter of John's gospel indicates how this message was received by some of his contemporaries: it was quite beyond them. They said, in a mixture of bewilderment and indignation: 'What are you talking about? We are free already

— we have the scriptures. Who is this Father you keep going on about? Abraham is our father'. And they attacked him with stones.

Not surprising really: the shock of the new always produces that kind of dull incomprehension and hostility. But what is surprising, and much more depressing, is that this contemporary reaction to Jesus described in the eighth chapter of John is just as much the reaction of a certain type of Christian mind. No sooner has Jesus opened the door, than this type of mind wants to slam it shut again. No sooner has Jesus liberated people from their servitude to a god of rules and regulations, and to the letter instead of the spirit, than this type of mind puts the Bible on a pedestal and begins to worship it instead. No sooner have people been given a vision of the true God, than they voluntarily subject themselves again to a pedestrian literalism.

Because the real trouble with the Fundamentalist is that he has no imagination. All the things I have been talking about — change, risk, openness, lateral thinking — all these things are the marks of creativity. A blind and slavish obedience to what already exists is the very opposite of creativity.

The Old Testament says that we are made in the image of God, and the New Testament says that we are called to freedom. This means that we are invited to imitate God's creativity and to share in it. I've just been reading a book in which the main character has only one wish for his children: 'Let them be original'. That, I am sure, is God's wish for us, that each of us should be original, in imitation of him.

God is the one who takes risks. You can see this in the abject specimens of humanity he singles out to fulfil his purposes — the cheats and liars and weaklings, like old Jacob and King David, and the apostle Paul. You can see it in that masterstroke of risk and imagination and lateral thinking, the incarnation, when God took it into his head to become a human baby — who else but God would ever have had that idea, or been willing to try it?

And God, in Jesus, is the one who is open, open to everyone, to criminals and whores and misfits. He comes not to call the righteous — in other words the orthodox believers, who can quote the scriptures and shelter behind them; instead of these he comes to call sinners, like the woman of the streets who poured out precious ointment and washed his feet with her hair. It was a crazy gesture, which aroused the horrified indignation of the Pharisee, but which has become an eternal symbol of the imaginative extravagance which lies at the heart of Christianity.

It is this kind of imaginative act that we are called to perform. The teaching of Jesus is full of similar challenges: the merchant is to sell everything to buy the one true pearl; the rich young man is to give away everything he has and follow Jesus; we are to put our hand to the plough and not look back; we must leave our dead to bury their dead; we must imitate the son of man in having no place to lay our heads; we must abandon everything — houses, families, possessions.

Always it is a question of risk. We must in principle be prepared to jettison everything; and that means not just material things, and not even mainly material things. It applies much more to the things of the mind, to our presuppositions, to the mental straitjacket which controls us. We can only really be open to God if we are prepared to accept the possibility that everything we think we know about him and about ourselves is mistaken. To be perfect is to have changed often.